FAMILY HISTORY
Logbook

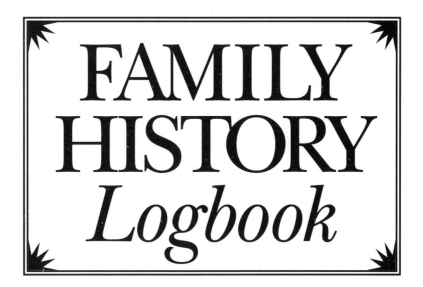

FAMILY HISTORY *Logbook*

REINHARD KLEIN

BETTERWAY BOOKS
CINCINNATI, OHIO

The Family History Logbook. Copyright © 1996 by Reinhard Klein. Printed and bound in the United States of America. All rights reserved. No part of this book may be reproduced in any form or by any electronic or mechanical means including information storage and retrieval systems without permission in writing from the publisher, except by a reviewer, who may quote brief passages in a review. Published by Betterway Books, an imprint of F&W Publications, Inc., 1507 Dana Avenue, Cincinnati, Ohio 45207. (800)289-0963. First edition.

Other fine Betterway Books are available from your local bookstore or direct from the publisher.

00 99 98 97 96   5 4 3 2 1

Library of Congress Cataloging-in-Publication Data

Klein, Reinhard
  The family history logbook / Reinhard Klein.—1st ed.
     p.   cm.
  ISBN 1-55870-425-6
  1.
PN 1996
792'.025—dc20   *96-22964*
                                     CIP

Editor: Argie J. Manolis
Production editor: Katie Carroll
Cover and interior designer: Angela Lennert Wilcox

Betterway Books are available for sales promotions, premiums and fund-raising use. Special editions or book excerpts can also be created to specification. For details, contact: Special Sales Manager, F&W Publications, 1507 Dana Avenue, Cincinnati, Ohio 45207.

For Brianna and Michael

Reinhard was born in West Germany in 1950 to parents of Folk German and Austrian ethnicity who were refugees from Hungary and the Carpathian Mountains (currently part of Ukrainia). The family emigrated to Chicago in the mid-1950s along with other Germans from his father's village in Hungary. Interest in foreign lands and cultures led Reinhard to pursue a degree in anthropology which was awarded in 1973 from Northern Illinois University. After a series of interesting jobs from 1965 through 1974, which included auto mechanic, archaeological field assistant, carnival concession manager, construction worker, and technical illustrator, Reinhard became a jeweler and practiced his craft until 1994, when he decided to pursue a degree in elementary education. He was awarded this degree in May, 1996. He currently resides in a small town in New Mexico with his wife and two children.

A few years ago my wife and I got the idea of making a timeline for my daughter to visually demonstrate how old she was compared to her parents and little brother. After completing the basic format, we found we weren't satisfied with just writing down the important events in our own lives, such as our birth dates, graduation dates, and the date of our marriage. As we worked on the timeline, we found it fun to comment on the individual years. For instance, when we were talking about 1969, my wife and I both recalled the day the first man walked on the moon. We then discussed other events that happened that same year, such as Woodstock. I recalled that I never really learned about Woodstock until the album and the movie came out a couple years later. Or did they come out right away? Maybe I wasn't paying attention to that aspect of popular culture. In 1969, I was too busy learning Korean karate on Clark Street in the old Andersonville section of Chicago. My wife said she was still in junior high at the time and only heard about Woodstock from her big brothers and friends. We came to the conclusion that we had different interpretations of what happened during that year.

Collective and Personal History

I became fascinated by the realization that there is a difference between our nation's collective history and our personal history. How we think of the past and the present is affected by our awareness of certain events. For example, it seems as though everyone talks and writes about the 1960s as though they personally were major players and manipulators of the events. For some reason I vacillated between being a cautious participant, to being merely an observer who was trying to make sense of what the heck was going on!

I remember the start of the 1960s with the election of J.F.K. to the presidency. I was ten years old at the time. What I remember best about the election is that some of our neighbors didn't approve of J.F.K. because he was Catholic. They believed that he would take orders from the Pope! In retrospect I suppose this was the beginning of my awareness of politics. The nuns in my parochial school held up J.F.K. as a positive role model of a good Catholic American and a good family man.

When he was assassinated in 1963 it was a terrible shock. We were all convinced it was a Russian/Cuban plot to weaken America. Then we heard rumors that gangsters were behind it, then C.I.A. involvement, then big business. Many of us felt and still do that we may never know what really happened.

I became a teenager also in 1963. My friends and I heard our parents and extended family joking about us becoming "crazy teenagers" who spent all their time listening to that wild music on the radio. "Is that what a teenager does?" I thought. "Well, since I'm a teenager, I better get with the program." I purchased an established consumer product, the pocket transistor radio with earphones, and tuned into music and ball games while the rest of the family talked about others things. I only did this for my family's benefit. When I was with my friends, we'd either have the music on very low and talk, or not have music on at all. In fact, when I had time to myself I read or fooled around with various ongoing projects rather than listening to music.

We lived a few miles from O'Hare airport in Chicago, in the middle of the dual approach airplane pathways. Toward the end of the 1960s, when the Democratic Convention was held in Chicago, I watched the happenings on TV. During the convention there were at least twenty jets visible at all times. Half of them were military troop transports bringing in the federal troops which Mayor Daley had requested. I knew that something big was going on, even though I did not attend or protest.

I worked part-time at my uncle's gas station that summer. Among the regular customers who were mainly World War II and Korean War vets, there was a lot of talk about respect for our country, and freedom, and why demonstrators should be beaten. There was also an editorial cartoon in the newspaper which showed two Chicago policemen talking about the Russian destruction of the "Prague Spring" and how those dirty commies imposed their will on others! The following fall in contemporary history class we saw a 16mm film which recorded the Chicago police as anything but the saviors of democracy. They were captured on film beating immobilized protestors and dragging them to the paddy wagons. This was a very different image than what the city and mayor were trying to portray. It was all very confusing for a young man of 18.

I don't want you to think my only reminiscences of the 1960s were political. I've got so many different stories to tell about the late 1960s, such as my first date, my first car, going to a drive-in movie, going to teenage dance clubs, cruisin', working on the car, making chains with pull-tabs before the pop-top was introduced, hangin' out at the Lake Michigan beaches during the day even though they were littered with millions of dead alewives, working in the evenings, coming home to get fed and get clean clothes. Summers were great! Fall, winter, and spring were for bowling, school and working out at the Y.

The 1960s was the time I joined my first organized sport, Little League. It wasn't until years later that I figured out that the fish and pork chop jokes between our two coaches were a friendly way of reconciling their religious differences! The nuns made us aware of the Civil Rights movement. We listened to Negro music so, we wondered, why shouldn't we associate with them? For that matter, why were Polish jokes so popular? Many of our neighbors and classmates were Polish and they were just as clever and hard working as everyone else. Italians joked about their supposed mafia and gang connections. The Irish joked about their city hall and political connections. What a city! What a time!

I graduated from high school in 1969 and went on to college. I was away from home for the first time by myself. The Vietnam war was raging, the war protests were getting more confrontational, the army was training troops for riot control, the "pill" became readily available, acid-rock was getting a toe-hold on our eardrums, the Black Panthers were working to build pride in the black community. There were rumors of LSD and psychedelic parties. There were beer busts, black light posters, bell bottoms, long hair and beards, short hair and shaves, bras being burned, America Love It or Leave It bumper stickers, a fledgling environmental movement. . . . Whoa! I think I'll stop right here because there was so much going on.

The Purpose of This Book

You may be thinking, "What is this guy talking about? None of this stuff happened to me. For one thing, I'm older. I was born right after World War II, and I lived in a different part of the country. I was too busy raising a family during the 1960s to worry about all that stuff! It wasn't until I retired a few years ago that I was able to take a breather and think about some of the events of those years."

Great! That's just my point. Your personal history is different from mine. Your personal history is unique, just as my brothers', who are nine and ten years younger than me. When most historians write about history, they write from a perspective of the collective or generalized history, something on the national level. You, however, can make history more relevant to your family by writing on a personal level, what you saw and how you interpreted the events which occurred during your lifetime.

True, some facts affected us similarly, like the moon landing. But how many of us bought into the Woodstock legend, or had the courage to protest the Vietnam war with riot police looking for any excuse to bust someone's head in? How many can talk about jungle combat and understand the meaning of putting your life on the line day in and day out? We all experienced the 1960s differently just as we experienced each year differently. The purpose of this book is to give you a place to record the events that made a difference in your own life, and to help you recall those news events and changes in popular culture that meant something to you.

This Book Is for You

This book is for the unsung heroes of our society, the ordinary people who will never be the subject of a made-for-TV movie or biography. That includes all of us who get up each morning, see the kids off, fight the traffic, make innumerable decisions at the workplace, run a few errands after work, feed the family, do a load of laundry, help with the homework, balance the checkbook, absorb the news, call mom and dad, read the kids a bedtime story, take a few minutes to talk with our partner, and plan the next day.

In the midst of this daily grind, you are faced with decisions every day—everything from what route to take to avoid highway construction, to which health insurance plan to take, to how to prioritize your time at work, to how to resolve an argument with your partner or child. These difficult decisions contribute to the stresses of modern life. You wonder if times were always this tough. You look to the future and realize that you will need to learn all types of new facts, skills and concepts to make yourself marketable in the rapidly changing workplace. You look to the past and think that things were easier in the "good old days."

After you've entered some information into this book and begun to use the facts presented to help you sort out our collective history, you will undoubtedly come to the realization that you have been making tough decisions your whole life. You may find that your life was affected by history and popular culture in ways you never realized. Things weren't really simpler and easier in the past—you just forgot about some of the times you went through. Events beyond your control, such as an illness or death in the family, may have made some periods in your life seem insurmountable. But you always regrouped, sought advice, got help and kept on living.

You probably found support in family and friends you have known since childhood or have met at work or through other professional, union, religious, political, civic or cultural organizations. Your involvement in such organizations and your connections with family members and friends have affected your life in many ways. You have accomplished a lot in your life, and yet in retrospect it seems so simple.

How to Use This Book

This book includes the years 1900-2000. A full two-page spread is devoted to each year. Each spread includes the following: A Historical Context section, which includes news events and changes in popular culture that occurred during that year; a large amount of blank space for recording the important events in your own life and the lives of relatives and friends; and a Catalog of Sources section to record your sources of information.

The Historical Context Section

The Historical Context section includes facts which I have collected from a number of sources, many of which are listed in the bibliography. I've chosen a wide range of topics which have had major affects on our collective history. Every year features a Headline briefly describing the watershed event of that year. I chose something to which most people with an understanding of history can relate, usually something that was covered widely in the media and had some effect on a wide variety of people.

Just as I've chosen the headlines, I've also chosen how to organize the information I felt would best describe that year. I've tried not to be repetitive by harping about a certain issue year after year. We all have our priorities and ideas about which issues and events are important and what we thought about them as they occurred. Some events were so well documented that they automatically made the list. The origins of other events were poorly documented and only became well known in later years as they became a part of our collective consciousness.

The Historical Context section details a variety of topics. Some may feel that I should have spent more time on serious topics such as crime or ecology and less on popular culture such as music, TV or film. I've tried to include a little something for everybody, a little something to spark the memory and get you to reflect on a whole variety of events. The generalized topics are Government, Military, Tragedy, Crime, Civil Rights, Labor, Education, Health, Organizations, Religion, Ecology, Exploration, Science, Inventions, New Products, Food, Transportation, Communication, Economics, Business, Books, Magazines, Newspapers, Theater, Art, Music, Dances, Radio, Film, TV, Fashion, Sports, Fads, Occasions, Notoriety, Fame, Miscellaneous and Population. These topics are self-explanatory and should make sense to almost anyone who was around at the time.

All the topics listed above organize the highlights of that particular year. They are intended to be sparks to ignite your memories of that period. Since the information for each year is limited, it would be helpful to look over a range of two years prior to and after the year in which you are interested. I've found that by the time I bought into a new product, or became aware of a particular lifestyle, it had been on the market for several years and had matured through several developmental phases. Take the computer, for instance. I didn't buy one until three years ago, well after the computer revolution supposedly took place.

Once a fact or topics has captured your interest for a certain year, you will no doubt wish to learn more about it. There are several ways to gather more information. Few individuals will help you more than your local librarian. In my quest for certain information I chased after librarians as they led me through mazes of shelves and dusty stacks of books. There are many fine sources available which summarize individual years or groups of years. Ask the reference librarian where to look.

Another valuable source of information is your local bookstore. It's definitely worth the investment to purchase a good book on a topic in which you are interested. Many bookstores now sell CD-ROMs which carry huge amounts of information. If you have a computer with a CD-ROM drive, it may be a more convenient way to access the information you are interested in than in buying a book.

Since we are now in the "age" of the "Information Superhighway" (is it really an age or just a blip on the time line?) there are thousands of sources on the Internet which will give you all kinds of information. Be careful about who is supplying the information. It's always best to take the time to double-check your sources. This goes for all sources, not just information you find on the Internet. I spent a lot of time confirming certain facts. Sometimes there were four different years cited in which an event was supposed to have ocurred. It took a lot of effort to come up with the correct dates.

The Catalog of Sources Section

There is a Catalog of Sources section for recording the location of your resource materials. Do not limit yourself when you think of materials. Use everything available to you, including photo albums, old 8mm film, cassette recordings, videotapes, diaries, letters and newspaper articles. This section also allows you to catalog any material which does not fit within the pages of this book.

The Open Space

Last of all there are two unlabeled blocks which you can use to enter your personal information, including the important milestones of your own life. You can include only the dates and brief descriptions of major events, or you may choose to elaborate on these events. You may also choose to use this space to write about events of facts of a collective nature that affected your life, such as milestones in sports, music or politics. You may find events that I left out which you want to include, or choose to elaborate on events already included.

How to Begin

The main idea behind this book is to leave a body of organized material about your life for future generations. The best way to begin writing your story is to take the simplest approach. Find a comfortable writing position and a good pencil and locate the year in which you were born. Enter your name, your parents' names, your birth date, your hometown and the country in which you were born. Now that you have broken the ice, enter another important event in your life—how about the year you got your first car, adopted your pets, moved, graduated from high school or college, started your first job, rented your first apartment, bought your house, or anything else you feel is significant and worthy of being recorded. Move from year to year in any order you like, because unlike life, which proceeds from beginning to end in a steady flow, your memory jumps around erratically. You may find it difficult to recall some of the milestones of your life because you probably haven't had time to reflect on these things for a while. You've been too busy living. As the weeks and months pass you will recall other important milestones as you continue with your story. Enter those events as they come to mind.

Now enter the names and milestones of other imme-diate family members just as you did for yourself. To do this, spend time talking to your partner and children about their lives. You may want to scour old photo albums or watch old family films or videos to remember these special events. If you do nothing else after this, you will have fulfilled the primary purpose of this book. You may wish to carry your project a step further, however.

Writing a Personal Narrative

Now that some of the major events of your life have been recorded, it's time for reflection. Pick a year onto which an entry was made. Read the facts for that year and surrounding years. Do they bring back memories? I'll bet they do. Jot down some of your areas of special interest, such as sports, art, music, politics or something else. When you have enough facts, write about an event that took place and color it with as many timely references as possible: the model car you drove, the pull-tab cans you drank from, searching for a "church key," the movies at the drive-in, the black-and-white TV shows, the radio program with the Top 40 countdown. Was your boyfriend about to get drafted? Did you just get a DA haircut like your buddies to match your black leather? Was your girlfriend sporting a Dorothy Hammil hairdo? Were your bobby socks rolled down for the proper effect? Did your parents finally give in that year and let you wear makeup?

You probably have enough details to easily write a 3,000 word story, and it couldn't possibly fit onto the space provided. Write your story on another sheet of paper, into a notebook, or on your computer. Your story could include photos or slides of the time the event took place. For example, you could make a special photo page illustrating the event. Title the paper and materials and label them clearly. Include a brief summary of your story on the page for that year. In the Catalog of Sources block, write down where the elaborated version and/or photos of the event can be found. You can develop a special filing system, including filing codes, to make record keeping easier. Congratulations! You have now put your first story into your book!

A problem which may arise is that most of us haven't written much more than Christmas cards, grocery lists or postcards for many years. That's still no excuse for not recording your contribution to history. Borrow a cassette deck, or rent a video recorder and tell your story. Imagine what it will be like forty years from now when your children or grandchildren watch or listen to this record! Once again, be sure to enter a brief summary of the recording and where you are storing it into this book.

Including Others in Your Story

After you have recorded a few personal narratives, you will realize that you were not alone when these important events in your life occurred. You had family and friends who were very active in your life. How do you include them? Browse through some of the memorabilia in your possession. There will be birth announcements, wedding invitations, forwarding addresses, holiday messages, letters from college or letters from the service. You will probably find lots of unexpected information and a way to make contact.

Interviewing relatives can be a fantastic experience or it can be extremely unnerving. You never know when you are going to accidently open some old wounds or repressed memories. With this in mind, think diplomatically, and be as reasonable and considerate as possible. Sometimes, because of family gossip, you know what not to talk about. Think of all the embarrassing moments that you would rather not talk about and that you hope no one remembers. Now put yourself in the place of your relative and think of how he would feel if you brought up a sore point. It's best to stick with topics of a very general nature and let the interviewee bring up subjects which may be taboo.

One personal unnerving incident which I encountered was back in 1973 during a European bicycle tour. I was visiting a second cousin in Heidelberg, West Germany. He brought me to his parents' home where I became acquainted with his grandmother. Somehow I ended up alone with her, and with a calm demeanor she began her tale with a moral: "Don't abandon your wife and children no matter how desperate the situation appears." It seems she married at the proper age for that society, about 17, and in quick succession gave birth to two children. Times being what they were, after World War I, there was no way to supplement their subsistence economy in their section of Austria-Hungary (now the Ukraine). Her husband left for America with assurances that he would send for the family once he got established. He did get established, but he never sent for his family. The extended family did help a little, but times were hard and she had to fend for herself and her two boys by doing all types of work from berry picking to laundry. She felt only bitterness for the man who had abandoned his sons and young wife. I didn't intend to interview anyone; I only happened to be in the right place at the right time and was offered a glimpse into my extended family's history. Be prepared to make some unexpected discoveries when you begin your investigations!

When interviewing someone, be patient, especially if they don't tell you right away what you think you want to know. If you are interviewing an uncle to get more information on one of your parents, be prepared to listen to a lot of information which has nothing to do with your questions. A standing joke in our family was not to let a certain uncle corner you because before you knew it he'd be telling you his life story beginning with how he left home in Yugoslavia for America and ended up bootlegging liquor to make a living. The car chases were legendary, in his mind at least, but he was always entertaining. According to my uncle, Prohibition made it possible for poor people to make a living and Al Capone was a hero to the poor. Since there was no welfare or social services, Capone sent food baskets to anyone who needed them. That is a far cry from the way the media portrays Al Capone! I guess the moral is you never know when a good story is going to come up. Be prepared to record it!

My maternal grandmother died a few weeks before she was to turn one-hundred. A few years before her death I had tried to gather some information about her life and times in what is now the Ukraine. I was disappointed when she showed little interest in my project. The next day Oma approached me with answers to most of my questions and I spent a wonderful hour listening to her stories. Looking back on the event I believe that she must have taken the time after our initial conversation to reflect on her life and compose answers to my questions. If you are going to interview someone, don't expect an immediate response to your questions. The questions you ask may be the farthest thing from their minds and they may need to reflect a bit before they can answer your questions. Once again, have your video camera ready.

Sometimes, when interviewing relatives you are comfortable around it may be necessary to go one-on-one with them even though a spouse will offer to "clarify" what the other is saying. To avoid having another person dominate the interview, find a place where you won't be disturbed so you can get the story straight from one person. You can always verify or refute what they said at a later date, through the other person.

Obtaining Information From Out-of-Town Relatives

In order to obtain the necessary information about your distant relatives it will be necessary to initiate contact with them. Mail your relatives a brief letter explaining that you are writing your family history and that you would like to include their histories along with yours. They will no doubt feel honored to be included in your story. Along with the explanation, enclose enough questionnaire forms for the family members residing at that address. As a thoughtful gesture, enclose a few extra questionnaire forms so they can make personal copies. Give them some time to respond, because, like you, they do have a life!

Before you send out a questionnaire like the following sample, it might be useful to offer an exchange of similar information. After all, wouldn't you be skeptical of someone asking for all kinds of personal information? Enclose a filled in questionnaire about yourself which you would like to share with them, and hopefully you'll be getting the same kind of information in return. Try not to get too personal with them at first, especially if they are several generations removed and you haven't had contact for many years.

After having established ties and sparked their curiosity you may wish to get together with them and record some stories of common interest. If you have been trying to write your story by following the sequence I've outlined, you may have found that it's easier to record stories on video- or cassette tapes than it is to write them out. Prepare yourself for the family encounter by having a recording device, charged battery pack, backup power cord and this book handy. It is best to prepare questions for the interview. Refer to your questionnaire as a starting point, and then use the Historical Context section to add questions, such as "How did you feel about the election of President Nixon?" or "Did your family celebrate the end of World War II?" Remember that the interviewee may stray from the questions. Do not let this bother you. Often the interviewee will give you useful information you never even thought of asking for. Share the information you have collected. Give them a copy of this book to complete themselves if they are especially enthusiastic and helpful.

Researching Your Family History

Even after talking with all living relatives, you may find several additional question marks about your family's history in the last one hundred years. This is when you may want to consider beginning a genealogical search by using resources like census records, deeds, newspapers, etc. *Unpuzzling Your Past* (by Emily Croom, published by Betterway Books), is an excellent starting point if you are interested in doing a more extensive search.

Using This Book as a Catalog of Archival Material

Some people, like me, have a partially organized collection of photos, letters, slides, tapes and other archival material. I'm waiting for this book to be published so that I can catalog all of that stuff in one central location. I'll use this book as the final catalog for all our memorabilia.

If you're an organized person, you probably either have a system in place for tracking your stuff or you can easily set one up. If, however, you're like the rest of us, you'll need some ideas to help you organize that stuff stuck under the bed, or on the top shelf of the bedroom closet. If you have a hodge-podge of stuff stuck here and there without any type of systematic organization, it's obvious that you would need to spend hours or even days figuring out a filing system for all your material. A task of this type can be daunting and will almost certainly be doomed to failure.

What I suggest is to gather some of the materials, photos, videotapes and newspaper clippings, and use them as the basis for a specific story. You can organize your story by attaching notes to the archival material. After enough notes and materials have been gathered for one good story, write down your story or record it on videotape. When you are satisfied that you have done enough for that particular event, put those materials in a large envelope or box. Label the container with the name of the person or persons the story is about, the year to which it refers, the year it was recorded, and an inventory of the container contents. For example, John James Doe, 1944, Pacific Theater war stories. Contains: 3 photos, 1 news clipping, videotape no. 8 of interview, 3-page summary of story. Put the same label information into the Catalog of Sources box of this book for the year 1944. You may then want to include a brief summary of the story in the space provided on the page. You have now cataloged a body of information and recorded a story which is important to you! Using this system, you'll probably end up with several boxes or envelopes for each year. They will all be neatly labeled and organized. This is just one suggestion for setting up an organizational system. You may want to find a method that works better for you.

Whatever method you use, make sure it is easy to locate slides, videos, cassette tapes, photos and other information for a particular year.

Organizing Your Photos

A good way to label a group photo is to label an enlarged photocopy of the group picture and keep the two together. I, for one, really need to do this. I keep thinking I'll remember all the people in our photographic collection, but I've already forgotten some individuals on slides I took only twenty-five years ago. All items in your files should have simple explanatory labels. I find that pencil works great because it allows you to make corrections if you find you've made an error. Keep everything simple and to the point.

Sometimes you will want to refer to the same photos, slides or videotapes several times. For most of us, duplicating this stuff becomes prohibitively expensive both in time and money. You can either do without the specific material or you can make a notation on your narratives where that material can be located. Don't make it too complicated or you'll never be able to piece it back together.

Some Final Ideas

When I was younger, I wasn't very interested in the stories older people had to tell; maybe they weren't very good storytellers, or maybe because I didn't have the sense of history and family that I do now. I was probably too busy trying to figure out how the world worked in my time, not my parents' time or grandparents' time. For example, my grandmother, who lived with us, was born before airplanes were invented. She had only four years of schooling in a foreign country. She didn't have a clue about American society and culture, and she had no way to make her life's experiences relevant to her grandchildren. But now I can see that many elements of her life were definitely worth recording and passing on. She and her husband had to guide their family through all types of experiences in Europe. When I think of her century of life and all she must have experienced, I become sad that I didn't take the time to listen to her stories and record them.

Think about the events in your life. Are those events only curiosities which made sense only during a certain period of our personal and collective history, or are there truths and morals which can be passed on to successive generations? With this idea in mind, write about the good times you had, the times when you made tough choices, and how you came through it all so you could offer some sage advice to your progeny!

Sample Questionnaire

Name (First, middle, last)
_____

Date of Birth
_____

Place of Birth
_____

Mother (include maiden name)
_____

Father
_____

If married, include date of marriage and name of spouse
_____
_____

If you have children, include their names, birth dates and current addresses:

Name
_____

Date of birth
_____

Address
_____
_____

Name
_____

Date of birth
_____

Address
_____
_____

Name
_____

Date of birth
_____

Address
_____
_____

Name
_____

Date of birth
_____

Address
_____
_____

Name
_____

Date of birth
_____

Address
_____

Who are some other relatives I should get in touch with?
_____
_____
_____
_____
_____
_____
_____
_____
_____
_____
_____
_____

If you wish, answer the following questions to provide me with more information about yourself:
Ethnic background(s):
_____
_____
_____

Jobs, careers and skills:
_____
_____
_____
_____
_____
_____

High school and college degrees, if any:

_____

_____

_____

_____

Hobbies and favorite activities:

_____

_____

_____

_____

_____

_____

_____

_____

_____

_____

_____

_____

_____

_____

Religious affiliation, if any:

_____

_____

_____

Organizations, if any:

_____

_____

_____

_____

List any milestones in your life which you would like to share:

_____

_____

_____

_____

_____

_____

_____

_____

Comments:

_____

_____

_____

_____

_____

_____

_____

1900

CATALOG *of Sources*

FAMILY
Milestones

HEADLINE: William McKinley and Theodore Roosevelt are elected president and VP. **GOVERNMENT**: Hawaii becomes a territory. ✴ The U.S. adopts the gold standard. **TRAGEDY**: Hurricane kills 6,000 in Galveston, TX. **LABOR**: The average work week is 59 hours. ✴ There are about 100,000 "lady typewriters" in the workplace. ✴ The International Ladies' Garment Workers Union is organized. **HEALTH**: Major Reed proves malaria is transmitted by mosquitoes. ✴ The average age of death of 47. **ORGANIZATIONS**: The first Junior League. **ACTIVISM**: Carry Nation and followers destroy saloons in Kansas. **ECOLOGY**: The U.S. has 30 head of bison. **INVENTIONS**: Kodak introduces the Brownie box camera. ✴ Hills Bros. begins packing ground roast coffee in tins. **TRANSPORTATION**: 144 miles of U.S. roads are hard-surfaced. **BOOKS**: *Lord Jim* by Joseph Conrad; *Sister Carrie* by Theodore Dreiser; *The Wizard of Oz* by L. Frank Baum; and *The Man That Corrupted Hadleyburg*, a short story by Mark Twain. **MUSIC**: A popular song is *A Bird in a Gilded Cage*. ✴ The player piano is a must-have in middle-class homes. **DANCES**: The Cake Walk is the popular dance. **FASHIONS**: Shirtwaists become fashionable. ✴ A lady's bicycling outfit may consist of a cotton bodice with a large bow, wool knickerbockers, black wool stockings, and leather lace-up boots. **SPORTS**: The five-sided home plate is introduced to baseball. ✴ The Davis Cup is established. **FAME**: Casey Jones dies on the doomed *Cannonball Express*. ✴ "The Great Houdini" begins his career. **MISCELLANEOUS**: The U.S. population is 75,994,575; one-third of all residents are foreign born; and 60 percent of the population is rural.

1901

FAMILY
Milestones

CATALOG of Sources

HISTORICAL *Context of 1901*

HEADLINE: President William McKinley is assassinated by Leon Czolgosz, an anarchist. Theodore Roosevelt is sworn in. **CIVIL RIGHTS**: President Roosevelt entertains Booker T. Washington at the White House. Some southern whites are outraged. ✳ Alabama adopts a new constitution which disenfranchises African-Americans. ✳ A circular from the Commission of Indian Affairs forbids religious dances and feasts, the wearing of long hair by men, face painting and Indian dress. **ORGANIZATIONS**: Victor L. Berger and Eugene V. Debs help found the American Socialist Party. **SCIENCE**: The National Bureau of Standards is established. ✳ Alfred L. Kroeber founds the Department of Anthropology at the University of California at Berkeley. **INVENTIONS**: K.C. Gillette begins producing the safety razor. **FOOD**: Satori Kato invents the first instant coffee. **BUSINESS**: U.S. Steel Corp. becomes the first billion-dollar corporation. ✳ Major oil discovery in TX. **BOOKS**: *The Octopus*, a novel by Frank Norris. **THEATER**: The Four Cohans appear in the musical, *The Governor's Son*. ✳ *If I Were King* by Justin Huntly McCarthy. **MUSIC**: Popular songs include *I Love You Truly*; *Boola Boola*; *Hello, Central, Give Me Heaven*; *The Easy Winners*. ✳ There are 13 major orchestras in the U.S. **SPORTS**: The first U.S. national bowling tournament is held. ✳ In baseball, the American League is formed to compete with the National League. **FADS**: A Ping-Pong craze sweeps the country. **MISCELLANEOUS**: Andrew Carnegie sells his company and devotes himself to philanthropy.

1902

CATALOG *of Sources*

FAMILY
Milestones

HEADLINE: John Mitchell leads 147,000 United Mine Workers on a strike that lasts five months. **GOVERNMENT**: Oliver Wendell Holmes is appointed to the U.S. Supreme Court. ✴ Bureau of the Census is established. ✴ U.S. acquires control of the unfinished Panama Canal. ✴ Roosevelt announces the end of the Philippine Insurrection. **HEALTH**: Dr. C.W. Stiles discovers the hookworm. ✴ Silver-gelatin colloid is used to prevent eye infections in newborns. ✴ An electric hearing aid is produced. **ORGANIZATIONS**: Carnegie Institution of Washington is founded. **ECOLOGY**: Roosevelt pushes for forest and water conservation. **INVENTIONS**: Rayon, the arc generator. **NEW PRODUCTS**: Crayola crayons and Barnum's Animal Crackers are introduced. ✴ Everyday deodorant is introduced for women. ✴ Sears, Roebuck & Co. catalog has 1,200 pages. **COMMUNICATION**: A telegraph cable is laid from California to Hawaii. **ECONOMICS**: Roosevelt institutes antitrust proceedings against various corporations. **BUSINESS**: Pepsi-Cola Co., F. W. Woolworth & Co., and Minnesota Mining & Manufacturing Co. start business. ✴ James Cash Penney opens a store in Kemmerer, WY. **BOOKS**: *The Virginian*, a novel by Owen Wister. ✴ "To Build a Fire," a short story by Jack London. **ART**: The Photo-Secession Group is founded by Alfred Stieglitz. ✴ Bronze sculpture: *Comin' Through the Rye* by Frederic Remington. **MUSIC**: *In the Good Old Summertime*; *Bill Bailey, Won't You Please Come Home*. **FASHIONS**: Some men's clothing costs include fancy suit, $9.00; work shoes, $1.25; linen collar, $.25. **SPORTS**: The first Tournament of Roses Association game (Rose Bowl). **FADS**: The teddy bear is introduced. **MISCELLANEOUS**: The comic strip "Buster Brown" debuts in the *New York Herald*.

1903

CATALOG *of Sources*

FAMILY *Milestones*

HISTORICAL *Context of 1903*

HEADLINE: Orville and Wilbur Wright complete the first successful airplane flight. **GOVERNMENT**: The Muckrakers expose corruption in politics. **MILITARY**: Panama declares its independence from Columbia after the U.S. cruiser *Nashville* provides assistance. **TRAGEDY**: 602 patrons die in the panic during a fire at Chicago's *Iroquois Theatre*. **CIVIL RIGHTS**: The U.S. Supreme Court upholds the Alabama Constitution denying African-Americans the right to vote. **LABOR**: 400 National Guardsmen move into Telluride, CO, to suppress the striking union. **HEALTH**: Mary Mallon, "Typhoid Mary," infects hundreds with typhoid. **ECOLOGY**: Pelican Island, FL, is the first national wildlife refuge. **INVENTIONS**: Michael Owens' bottle blowing machine begins production. **FOOD**: Sanka introduces instant decaffeinated coffee. **TRANSPORTATION**: A Packard car crosses the U.S. in 52 days. ✳ The Harley-Davidson motorcycle is introduced. **COMMUNICATION**: The first cable message is sent around the world. **ECONOMICS**: U.S. Supreme Court approves federal power to regulate commerce. ✳ Oil is discovered in Oklahoma Indian territory. **BUSINESS**: Henry Ford creates Ford Motor Company. ✳ Milton Hershey builds a chocolate factory outside of Harrisburg, PA. **BOOKS**: Novels: *The Pit* by Frank Norris; *The Call of the Wild* by Jack London; *Rebecca of Sunnybrook Farm* by Kate Douglas Wiggin. Helen Keller publishes her autobiography, *The Story of My Life*. **MUSIC**: *Sweet Adeline* is a popular song. ✳ Enrico Caruso makes his American debut. **FILM**: *The Great Train Robbery* shocks audiences when actor George Barnes fires a pistol at the camera. **SPORTS**: The Boston Red Sox defeat the Pittsburgh Pirates in the first World Series. ✳ Boxer Jim Jeffries defeats Jim Corbett.

1904

CATALOG *of Sources*

FAMILY *Milestones*

HEADLINE: Theodore Roosevelt and C.W. Fairbanks elected president and VP. **TRAGEDY**: 1,021 Sunday school picnickers die when the steamship *General Slocum* bursts into flame. ✳ Fire in Baltimore, MD, destroys 2,600 buildings. **CRIME**: A woman in New York City is arrested for smoking cigarettes in public. **CIVIL RIGHTS**: Reformers organize the National Child Labor Committee. **HEALTH**: William C. Gorgas begins a study to eliminate yellow fever. **ORGANIZATIONS**: The American Academy of Arts and Letters is founded. **ECOLOGY**: A Japanese exhibit at the New York Botanical Garden introduces a blight which begins to wipe out the American Chestnut tree. **INVENTIONS**: First diesel engine exhibited in U.S. **FOOD**: Syrian immigrant Ernest A. Hamwi invents the ice cream cone at the St. Louis fair. **TRANSPORTATION**: World's first underground and underwater railway opens in New York City. ✳ New York passes the first automobile speed law. **ECONOMICS**: The U.S. becomes the world's largest auto producer. **BUSINESS**: Montgomery Ward mails out 3 million free catalogs. **BOOKS**: Novels include *The Sea Wolf* by Jack London; *The Golden Bowl* by Henry James. **THEATER**: *The Little Minister*, a play by J.M. Barrie. **MUSIC**: *Meet Me in St. Louis, Louis*; *Give My Regards to Broadway*; *Frankie and Johnny* are popular songs. **SPORTS**: St. Louis, MO, hosts the World Exhibition and the Olympics where basketball is played as a demonstration game. ✳ "Cy" Young pitches the first perfect game. ✳ The International Pro Hockey League is formed. ✳ The Federation of International Football Association is formed to standardize soccer play. **MISCELLANEOUS**: Roosevelt is instructed in jujitsu.

1905

CATALOG *of Sources*

FAMILY *Milestones*

HISTORICAL *Context of 1905*

HEADLINE: A yellow fever epidemic, which kills 400, and a malaria epidemic, which kills 1,000, strike New Orleans. **ORGANIZATIONS**: American labor leader Eugene V. Debs founds the Industrial Workers of the World. ✴ First Rotary Club is formed. ✴ The Society of Automotive Engineers (SAE) is founded. ✴ The Niagara Movement is formed to demand full civil rights for African-Americans. **ECOLOGY**: Roosevelt creates a Bureau of Forestry to protect public lands. ✴ National Audubon Society forms. **SCIENCE**: Mount Wilson Observatory is completed. **INVENTIONS**: The first neon lights appear. **NEW PRODUCTS**: Introduction of Vicks VapoRub and Palmolive soap. **TRANSPORTATION**: 17,988 autos are registered in U.S. **BUSINESS**: L.C. Smith & Brothers sells its first typewriter. **BOOKS**: Novels include *White Fang* by Jack London and *The House of Mirth* by Edith Wharton. **NEWSPAPERS**: *The Chicago Defender* is launched. **THEATER**: *The Girl of the Golden West*. **MUSIC**: *My Gal Sal*; *In My Merry Oldsmobile*. **FASHIONS**: Ladies' hats must be elaborately feathered. **SPORTS**: The New York Giants defeat the Philadelphia Athletics in the World Series. ✴ Because of 18 deaths in college football this year the forerunner of the NCAA is founded. **NOTORIETY**: Zion, IL, comes under the control of Wilbur Glenn Voliva, a proponent of the "Flat Earth Theory." He unsuccessfully predicts the end of the world for 1923, 1927, 1930 and 1935. **FAME**: Alice Roosevelt, T.R.'s spirited daughter, announces her engagement. She is considered by many to be the embodiment of the "Gibson Girl." ✴ Will Rogers debuts in New York City. ✴ First cigarette testimonials by celebrities.

1906

CATALOG *of Sources*

FAMILY *Milestones*

HEADLINE: U.S. troops occupy Cuba. **GOVERNMENT**: Muckraker books *The Jungle* by Upton Sinclair and *The Great American Fraud* by Samuel H. Adams create such a public outcry that Congress passes the Pure Food and Drugs Act. **TRAGEDY**: A San Francisco earthquake leaves 500,000 homeless and kills 700. **HEALTH**: Patent medicines are required to declare narcotics content. **ORGANIZATIONS**: The American Jewish Committee is founded. ✳ The National Education Association incorporates. **INVENTIONS**: Willis Carrier patents his air conditioner. ✳ Victor Talking Machine Co. introduces the *Victrola*. **NEW PRODUCTS**: Introduction of Lux Flakes. **FOOD**: Planters Nut and Chocolate Co. is founded. ✳ Cocaine is removed from the Coca-Cola recipe. **COMMUNICATION**: Lee DeForest invents the vacuum tube. ✳ The first radio program with voice and music is broadcast. ✳ Anarchist Emma Goldman founds the journal *Mother Earth*. **BOOKS**: "The Gift of the Magi" by O. Henry and *The Spirit of the Border* by Zane Grey are published. **MUSIC**: *You're a Grand Old Flag*, *King Porter Stomp*, and *Anchors Aweigh* are popular songs. **FASHIONS**: Spalding introduces the saddle shoe. **SPORTS**: The forward pass is introduced in football. ✳ Chicago White Sox defeat the Chicago Cubs to take the World Series. ✳ The National Collegiate Athletic Association (NCAA) is formed. **NOTORIETY**: Harry Thaw kills noted architect Stanford White for having an affair with his wife, actress Evelyn Nesbit. It becomes the scandal of the decade. **MISCELLANEOUS**: Devils Tower National Monument and Mesa Verde National Park are created. **POPULATION**: More Americans, per capita, are addicted to narcotics than at any other time in U.S. history.

1907

FAMILY Milestones

CATALOG *of Sources*

HISTORICAL *Context of 1907*

HEADLINE: The bank panic and depression of 1907-08 begins. **GOVERNMENT**: Oklahoma enters the Union as the 46th state. **MILITARY**: "Great White Fleet" sails around world in show of strength. ✻ U.S. Marines sent to Honduras. **TRAGEDY**: A fire at Coney Island causes $1.5 million in property damage. **LABOR**: WFM leader "Big Bill" Haywood is acquitted of the murder of former Idaho governor Frank R. Steunenberg. **EDUCATION**: The IQ test is introduced. **ECOLOGY**: Roosevelt creates 16 million acres of national forest. **NEW PRODUCTS**: Introduction of Armstrong linoleum. **ECONOMICS**: J.P. Morgan holds 125 New York financiers under lock and key until they produce the capital to save the U.S. from financial collapse. **BOOKS**: *The Education of Henry Adams* by Henry Adams and "The Last Leaf," a story by O. Henry, are published. **THEATER**: The *Ziegfeld Follies of 1907*. **ART**: Julian & Maria Martinez of San Ildefonso Pueblo, NM, begin experimenting with black-on-black pottery. ✻ The first volume of *The North American Indian* by Edward S. Curtis. **MUSIC**: Popular songs include *School Days* and *The Caissons Go Rolling Along*. **SPORTS**: Cooperstown, NY, is declared the birthplace of baseball. ✻ The Chicago Cubs defeat the Detroit Tigers to take the World Series. **OCCASIONS**: The first Mother's Day is observed. **NOTORIETY**: Annette Kellerman, a long-distance swimmer, is arrested for indecent exposure while in a skirtless one-piece bathing suit. **FAME**: Florence Lawrence (the Biograph Girl) is the first film star. ✻ Rube Goldberg begins his cartooning career with the *New York Evening Journal*. **POPULATION**: 1.29 million new immigrants.

1908

FAMILY
Milestones

HEADLINE: William H. Taft and James S. Sherman elected president and VP. **MILITARY**: Wilbur Wright delivers a flying machine to the War Department. **CRIME**: New York City prohibits smoking in public by women. **CIVIL RIGHTS**: The National Association for the Advancement of Colored People (NAACP) is founded. **HEALTH**: First Red Cross Christmas seals. ✳ Introduction of disposable paper cups. **INVENTIONS**: Electric iron and toaster are patented. **TRANSPORTATION**: U.S. begins construction of the "Big Ditch," the Panama Canal. ✳ Henry Ford introduces the Model T. **BUSINESS**: Du Pont Company begins production of plastics. ✳ Automaker William Durant founds the General Motors Company. **BOOKS**: Novels include *The Last of the Plainsmen* by Zane Grey and *Anne of Green Gables* by Lucy M. Montgomery. **NEWSPAPERS**: The *Christian Science Monitor* begins publication. **ART**: The Ashcan School of painters exhibit in New York City. **MUSIC**: *Shine On, Harvest Moon*; *Cuddle Up a Little Closer*; *Take Me Out to the Ball Game*. **DANCE**: Original performances by Isadora Duncan set new standards in dance. **FILM**: The National Board of Censorship forms to police the film industry. **FASHIONS**: Sheath gowns, fish-net stockings, and boned collars are fashionable women's wear. **SPORTS**: The Chicago Cubs defeat the Detroit Tigers to take the World Series. ✳ Figure skating arrives from Europe. ✳ George Schuster wins the New York-to-Paris motorcar race. ✳ Jack Johnson becomes the first African-American heavyweight boxing champion. **MISCELLANEOUS**: "Mutt and Jeff" comics appear in the *San Francisco Examiner*. ✳ The steerage rate from Genoa, Italy to New York City is $12.

1909

CATALOG *of Sources*

FAMILY *Milestones*

HISTORICAL *Context of 1909*

HEADLINE: Robert E. Peary "discovers" the North Pole. **MILITARY**: Nicaragua's president is ousted by U.S. Marines. **LABOR**: Japanese workers stage the first major Hawaiian labor strike. ✶ 20,000 U.S. garment workers belonging to the Ladies' Waist Makers' Union Local 25 begin a three-month strike. **HEALTH**: Opium smoking is made illegal, but it is still legal in patent medicines. **SCIENCE**: Aaron Levene discovers RNA in cell nuclei. **INVENTIONS**: Leo Baekeland develops Bakelite, which begins the age of plastic. **COMMUNICATION**: First wireless message sent from New York City to Chicago. ✶ The U.S. copyright law takes effect. **BOOKS**: Novels include *A Girl of Limberlost* by Gene Stratton Porter and *Martin Eden* by Jack London. ✶ Poetry collections include *Poems* by William Carlos Williams. **THEATER**: *The Melting Pot* by Israel Zangwill introduces the term "melting pot." **ART**: George Bellows paints the prize fight scene *Stag at Sharkey's*. **MUSIC**: *Put on Your Old Grey Bonnet* and *Casey Jones* are popular songs. **FILM**: *Gertie the Dinosaur* is the first notable animated cartoon. **FASHIONS**: A suntanned "Outdoor Girl" replaces the pale "Gibson Girl." **SPORTS**: Philadelphia builds the first modern ballpark. ✶ The Pittsburgh Pirates defeat the Detroit Tigers to take the World Series. ✶ Louis Stang averages 64 mph to win the 100-mile Indianapolis race. ✶ Glenn H. Curtiss wins the first international air race at Reims, France. **FADS**: Kewpie dolls first appear as illustrations in the *Ladies' Home Journal*. **MISCELLANEOUS**: Frank Lloyd Wright's Robie House in Chicago is completed. ✶ The Philadelphia Mint issues the Lincoln penny.

1910

CATALOG *of Sources*

FAMILY
Milestones

HISTORICAL *Context of 1910*

HEADLINE: Halley's comet harmlessly passes earth. **MILITARY**: The first aircraft takes off from a U.S. warship. **CRIME**: Fugitive Dr. Crippen is the first murderer trapped by wireless (radio). ✶ The newly enacted Mann Act prohibits interstate transportation of women for "immoral purposes." **LABOR**: The average U.S. worker works 54 to 60 hours per week. **ORGANIZATIONS**: The Campfire Girls and Boy Scouts of America are founded. **SCIENCE**: Thomas Morgan develops a gene theory which earns him a Nobel Prize. **NEW PRODUCTS**: Electric cooking ranges and washing machines are introduced. **FOOD**: 70 percent of U.S. bread is home-baked. **ECONOMICS**: The Fidelity Loan and Trust Co., the first "Morris Plan" bank, grants personal loans to good credit risks on monthly installments. **BUSINESS**: The Fuller Brush Co. is incorporated. ✶ *Women's Wear Daily* begins publication. **THEATER**: The Broadway musical *Naughty Marietta* opens. **MUSIC**: *Mother Machree*; *Come, Josephine, In My Flying Machine*; *Down by the Old Mill Stream*; *Let Me Call You Sweetheart*. ✶ Tin Pan Alley sells two billion copies of sheet music. **FILM**: *Ramona* with Mary Pickford is a smash hit. ✶ Cartoonist John Randolph Bray pioneers animated cartoons using the cel system. ✶ The film studios adopt the "star system" to promote films. **FASHIONS**: The hobble skirt is the rage. **SPORTS**: The Philadelphia Athletics defeat the Chicago Cubs to take the World Series. ✶ Barney Oldfield sets speed record of 131 mph. **OCCASIONS**: The first Father's Day is observed. **MISCELLANEOUS**: Glacier National Park is created. **POPULATION**: U.S. population 91,972,266. ✶ The great migration of African-Americans from south to north begins.

1911

FAMILY
Milestones

HEADLINE: 146 sweatshop workers die in the Triangle Shirtwaist Co. fire. Large numbers of garment workers join unions. **GOVERNMENT**: The Supreme Court breaks up the Standard Oil Company trust. **MILITARY**: U.S. sends 20,000 troops to Mexican border. ✳ American Samuel Zemurray sets up a new "banana republic" in Honduras with the aid of soldiers of fortune Guy "Machine Gun" Molony and Lee Christmas. **ORGANIZATIONS**: The Carnegie Corporation is created. **EXPLORATION**: Hiram Bingham discovers the lost Inca city of Machu Picchu. **INVENTIONS**: Browning automatic pistol. ✳ Gulf Oil establishes offshore oil drilling. **FOOD**: *Crisco* is introduced by Procter & Gamble. **TRANSPORTATION**: First cross-country flight, from New York to California. ✳ GM introduces the electric self-starter. **BUSINESS**: IBM incorporates after consolidation with other companies. ✳ Chevrolet Motor Co. is founded. **MAGAZINES**: The magazine *Masses* is founded. **ART**: *The Geranium*, a painting by Max Weber. **MUSIC**: *Alexander's Ragtime Band*; *Memphis Blues*; *Goodnight Ladies*; *Oh, You Beautiful Doll*; *My Melancholy Baby*; *I Want a Girl Just Like the Girl that Married Dear Old Dad*. **DANCES**: The Turkey Trot is popular. **FILM**: The first film studio is established in Hollywood, CA. **SPORTS**: The Philadelphia Athletics defeat the Chicago Cubs to take the World Series. ✳ A. Marmon Wasp wins the Indianapolis 500 with an average speed of 75 mph. ✳ Jim Thorpe leads the Carlisle Indian School to beat Harvard 18-15. **FADS**: *Submerged Atlantis Restored* is claimed to have been written with the help of departed Atlantean souls contacted through spirit mediums. **FAME**: Ishi, the last survivor of the Yahi tribe, walks into Oroville, CA.

1912

CATALOG *of Sources*

FAMILY
Milestones

HISTORICAL *Context of 1912*

HEADLINE: *Titanic* strikes iceberg and sinks; 1,500 perish. **GOVERNMENT**: Woodrow Wilson and Thomas R. Marshall elected president and V.P. **MILITARY**: U.S. troops sent to Nicaragua, Cuba and China. **LABOR**: Congress grants the 8-hour workday to federal employees. **EDUCATION**: The Montessori philosophy of education is popularized. **MEDICINE**: The *Journal of the American Medical Association* (JAMA) gives the first descriptive diagnosis of a heart attack. ✷ The discovery of vitamins A and B. **ORGANIZATIONS**: National American Women's Suffrage Association organizes to campaign for equal rights for women. ✷ Juliette Gordon Low starts the first troop of Girl Guides (Girl Scouts) in Savannah, GA. ✷ Henrietta Szold founds Hadassah. **FOOD**: Hellmann's Blue Ribbon Mayonnaise and Oreo Biscuits are introduced. **COMMUNICATION**: The SOS is adopted as the universal distress signal. **BUSINESS**: Cracker Jack puts toy surprises in bags of caramel-coated popcorn. ✷ The first self-service grocery stores open in California. **BOOKS**: *Tarzan of the Apes*, a novel by Edgar Rice Burroughs. **ART**: Paintings: *McSorley's Bar* and *Sunday, Women Drying Their Hair* by John F. Sloan. **MUSIC**: Leopold Stokowski becomes conductor of the Philadelphia Symphony Orchestra. ✷ *Moonlight Bay*, *That Old Gang of Mine*, and *When Irish Eyes are Smiling* are popular. **DANCES**: The castle waltz, bunny hop, fox-trot and grizzly bear. **FILM**: *Queen Elizabeth*; *Her First Biscuit* with Mary Pickford. **SPORTS**: American Indian Jim Thorpe wins the Olympic decathlon and pentathlon. ✷ The Boston Red Sox defeat the New York Giants to take the World Series. ✷ Open nets are introduced to basketball. ✷ First successful parachute jump. **MISCELLANEOUS**: New Mexico and Arizona enter the Union as the 47th and 48th states.

1913

FAMILY
Milestones

HEADLINE: 5,000 demonstrating suffragettes are assaulted by men who slap, spit at, and poke them with lighted cigars. **GOVERNMENT**: 16th Amendment to the Constitution establishes federal income tax, 17th Amendment provides for direct election of U.S. Senators. **LABOR**: The U.S. Department of Labor is created. **HEALTH**: John D. Rockefeller founds Rockefeller Institute with $1 million **ORGANIZATIONS**: Marcus Garvey founds the Universal Negro Improvement Association. ✴ The Anti-Defamation League and the American Cancer Society are founded. **INVENTIONS**: The modern X-ray tube is invented. **NEW PRODUCTS**: A home refrigerator and Brillo pads are introduced. **FOOD**: Quaker's Puffed Rice, Quaker's Puffed Wheat and Peppermint Life Savers are introduced. **TRANSPORTATION**: Ford sets up an assembly line to produce the Model T. **COMMUNICATION**: U.S. Parcel Post service begins. **ECONOMICS**: The Federal Reserve System is created. **BOOKS**: *Pollyanna*, a novel by Eleanor Porter. **ART**: The Armory Show introduces cubism and post-impressionism to New York. **MUSIC**: *Ballin' the Jack, Peg o' My Heart*, and *If I Had My Way*. **SPORTS**: The Philadelphia Athletics defeat the New York Giants to take the World Series. ✴ Notre Dame defeats Army through innovative use of the forward pass. **FADS**: The food-fad book: *Fletcherism: What It Is, or, How I Became Young at Sixty*. ✴ Kewpie dolls and crossword puzzles are instant successes. **OCCASIONS**: Civil War reunion at Gettysburg. **NOTORIETY**: Cecil B. DeMille is shot at twice by snipers hired by rival movie companies. **MISCELLANEOUS**: Camel cigarettes feature "Old Joe," a camel from the Barnum & Bailey circus.

1914

CATALOG *of Sources*

FAMILY *Milestones*

HEADLINE: World War I begins; U.S. declares neutrality. **GOVERNMENT**: U.S. ships $5 million in gold to Europe to aid stranded Americans. **MILITARY**: U.S. Marines occupy Veracruz, Mexico. **LABOR**: Ford announces a $5-a-day minimum wage. ✷ Joe Hill is convicted of the murder of a Salt Lake City grocer and his son. ✷ In the Ludlow Massacre, 2 women, 11 children and 8 men are killed as striking miners battle state militia near Trinidad, CO. **ORGANIZATIONS**: The national 4-H Club is founded. **ECOLOGY**: Last passenger pigeon dies at Cincinnati Zoo. **SCIENCE**: Robert H. Goddard begins rocketry experiments. ✷ George Washington Carver begins publicizing the results of his agricultural experiments. **INVENTIONS**: Corning Glass Works introduces Pyrex. ✷ Cadillac develops the V-8 engine. **TRANSPORTATION**: The Panama Canal opens to traffic. **COMMUNICATION**: Coast-to-coast telephone service is begun. **BOOKS**: *Penrod* by Booth Tarkington, *The Eyes of the World* by Harold Bell Wright and *North of Boston* by Robert Frost. **MUSIC**: *St. Louis Blues*; *By the Beautiful Sea*; *A Little Bit of Heaven* are popular songs. **FILM**: *The Perils of Pauline*, a serial in which each episode ends in a cliff-hanger. ✷ Other films include *Between Showers* and *Tillie's Punctured Romance* ✷ Mary Pickford signs a film contract with Adolph Zukor for $2,000 a week. **FASHIONS**: Mary Phelps Jacob patents the elastic brassiere. **SPORTS**: Walter Hagen wins the U.S. Open. ✷ The Boston Braves defeat the Philadelphia Athletics to take the World Series. **FADS**: The Chautauqua Movement combines popular entertainment with inspirational lectures for personal success. **MISCELLANEOUS**: Paul Bunyan and Babe are created for promotional literature.

1915

CATALOG *of Sources*

FAMILY
Milestones

HISTORICAL *Context of 1915*

HEADLINE: German U-boats sink U.S. merchant ships carrying war contraband to England. Among those sunk is the passenger ship *Lusitania*. **GOVERNMENT**: The U.S. recognizes the Mexican government of Venustiano Carranza. **MILITARY**: U.S. Marines occupy Haiti. ✳ U.S. Coast Guard established. **CIVIL RIGHTS**: Margaret Sanger is imprisoned for her birth control book *Family Limitation*. **LABOR**: Labor organizer Joe Hill is executed by firing squad. **HEALTH**: Tests on volunteer inmates in Mississippi demonstrate that pellagra is the result of diet deficiency. **ECOLOGY**: Congress creates Rocky Mountain National Park. **INVENTIONS**: The Thompson submachine gun is invented. **FOOD**: Kraft introduces processed cheese. **TRANSPORTATION**: Ford produces his 1 millionth automobile. **COMMUNICATION**: The 78 rpm record becomes the main source of recorded music. **ECONOMICS**: U.S. bankers loan France and England $500 millon. **BUSINESS**: Metropolitan Life Insurance becomes a mutual company. **BOOKS**: *A Spoon River Anthology* by Edgar Lee Masters and *Chicago Poems* by Carl Sandburg are published. **ART**: The Dada art and literary movement begins. **MUSIC**: *I Didn't Raise My Boy to Be a Soldier*; *Pack Up Your Troubles in Your Old Kit Bag*; *M-O-T-H-E-R, a Word that Means the World to Me*. **DANCES**: Boston bans the turkey trot, bunny hug and grizzly bear. **FILM**: Films include *Birth of a Nation*, by D.W. Griffith, *A Fool There Was* with Theda "The Vamp" Bera. **FASHIONS**: Lipstick becomes commercially available. **SPORTS**: Jess Willard takes the heavyweight title from Jack Johnson. ✳ The Boston Red Sox defeat the Philadelphia Phillies to take the World Series. **NOTORIETY**: William J. Simmons revives the Ku Klux Klan.

1916

FAMILY
Milestones

CATALOG *of Sources*

HISTORICAL *Context of 1916*

HEADLINE: Woodrow Wilson and Thomas R. Marshall reelected president and VP. **GOVERNMENT**: Congress creates the U.S. National Park Service and the Federal Farm Loan Board. **MILITARY**: Pancho Villa and his band raid Columbus, NM; General Pershing and troops pursue him. ✷ The U.S. National Defense Act prepares the U.S. for war. **TRAGEDY**: 28,000 are struck by a polio outbreak. **CIVIL RIGHTS**: Jeanette Rankin of Montana is the first woman elected to U.S. House. ✷ Margaret Sanger opens the first birth control clinic and is promptly arrested. **LABOR**: Federal employees are protected by a Workmen's Compensation Act. **HEALTH**: Frederick S. Motley discovers that fluoride salts in drinking water prevent cavities. **RELIGION**: Father Divine organizes the Peace Mission Movement. **ECOLOGY**: The Japanese beetle appears in America. **HOUSEHOLD**: Converse basketball shoes and U.S. Keds are introduced. ✷ Coca-Cola introduces its distinctive bottle design. ✷ Piggly-Wiggly becomes the first supermarket chain. **TRANSPORTATION**: Congress passes a Federal Highway Act to promote highway construction. **BOOKS**: *Seventeen*, a novel by Booth Tarkington; *The Road Not Taken*, a collection of poetry by Robert Frost and *You Know Me Al* by Ring Lardner are published. **ART**: Norman Rockwell begins illustrating for the *Saturday Evening Post*. **MUSIC**: *I Ain't Got Nobody* and *La Cucaracha* are released. **FILM**: *Intolerance* by D.W. Griffith. **SPORTS**: Professional golfers establish the PGA. ✷ R. Norris Williams takes the U.S. Open Tennis Championship. ✷ The Boston Red Sox defeat the Brooklyn Dodgers to take the World Series. **NOTORIETY**: Hetty Green, "the witch of Wall Street," dies. **MISCELLANEOUS**: "Mr. Peanut" makes his debut at Planters.

1917

CATALOG *of Sources*

FAMILY *Milestones*

CATALOG *of Sources*

HISTORICAL *Context of 1917*

HEADLINE: The U.S. declares war on Germany and Austria-Hungary. **GOVERNMENT**: The Virgin Islands and Puerto Rico become U.S. territories. **MILITARY**: The convoy system reduces Allied losses to German submarines. ✳ The Zimmermann note proposing a secret Mexican alliance with Germany is revealed. ✳ Selective Service Act. ✳ A recruiting poster shows Uncle Sam pointing his finger and saying, "I Want You." **CIVIL RIGHTS**: Suffragettes arrested for picketing in front of the White House. **LABOR**: American women begin to take on "men's" work as the men are sent to fight in Europe. ✳ 1,100 Wobbly miners on strike in Bisbee, AZ, are held in a stockade by the U.S. army. ✳ U.S. government takes over the railroads. **INVENTIONS**: An automated plate glass machine designed by Michael Owens begins production. **BUSINESS**: Union Carbide and Phillips Petroleum are formed. **BOOKS**: *The Innocents*, a novel by Sinclair Lewis. ✳ The first Pulitzer Prizes are awarded for best novel, play, history and biography. **THEATER**: The Empire Theater in Montgomery, AL, installs air-conditioning. **MUSIC**: Violinist Jascha Heifetz makes his U.S. debut. ✳ Jelly Roll Morton, Sidney Bechet, Bunk Johnson and Louis Armstrong make their way to Chicago. ✳ *Over There*; *Jelly Roll Blues*; *You're in the Army Now*; *Hail, Hail, the Gang's All Here*; *Tiger Rag*. **FILM**: *The Little Princess* with Mary Pickford. **SPORTS**: The Chicago White Sox defeat the New York Giants to take World Series. ✳ The NHL is organized. **FADS**: *Zone Therapy*, a quack medical book by Benedict Lust. **MISCELLANEOUS**: Introduction of the *World Book* encyclopedia. **POPULATION**: Puerto Ricans are given the right to U.S. citizenship.

1918

CATALOG *of Sources*

FAMILY *Milestones*

HISTORICAL *Context of 1918*

HEADLINE: U.S. troops turn the tide in WWI. Austria-Hungary and Germany sign armistice treaty. **GOVERNMENT**: Victor Berger is denied his seat in the U.S. House until the Supreme Court rules to seat him. ✶ President Wilson announces his Fourteen Points peace plan to counter the Bolshevik revelation of secret Allied plans to carve up the German Empire. **TRAGEDY**: Influenza epidemic kills 500,000 in U.S. and 20 million world wide. **LABOR**: The Supreme Court rules the Child Labor Law of 1916 unconstitutional in favor of states' rights. **RELIGION**: The Native American Church incorporates in Oklahoma. ✶ Aimee Semple McPherson founds the International Church of the Four-Square Gospel in Los Angeles. **SCIENCE**: Astronomer Harlow Shapley determines the dimensions of the Milky Way. **NEW PRODUCTS**: The first automatic pop-up toaster is patented. **FOOD**: Food is rationed in the U.S. to help the war effort. **TRANSPORTATION**: Fruehauf Trailer Co. is founded. **COMMUNICATION**: Airmail service begins in selected cities. ✶ Robert Lee Ripley begins *Believe It or Not*. **BOOKS**: Novels include *The Magnificent Ambersons* by Booth Tarkington, and *Raggedy Ann Stories* by Johnny Gruelle. **THEATER**: *Yip, Yip, Yaphank*, a wartime musical. **MUSIC**: *Mammy*; *I'm Forever Blowing Bubbles*; *Rock-a-bye Your Baby with a Dixie Melody*; *K-K-K-Katy*. **FILM**: *Shoulder Arms* with Charlie Chaplin; *When a Woman Sins* with Theda Bera. **SPORTS**: Knute Rockne begins coaching at Notre Dame. ✶ Boston Red Sox defeat the Chicago Cubs to take the World Series. **FADS**: The Raggedy Ann doll is introduced. **MISCELLANEOUS**: Dr. Littlefield invents the "Rainbow Lamp," a device he claims will cure many illnesses.

1919

FAMILY Milestones

CATALOG of Sources

CATALOG of Sources

HISTORICAL *Context of 1919*

HEADLINE: Emma Goldman and Alexander Berkman along with 200 other "Reds" are deported to Russia. **GOVERNMENT**: The U.S. Senate fails to ratify the Treaty of Versailles. ✳ Race riots in 26 U.S. cities. **TRAGEDY**: Goodyear balloon, the *Wing Foot*, crashes into a Chicago bank killing 12 and injuring 28. **LABOR**: Communist Labor Party is formed. ✳ Labor unrest in the U.S. as four million workers strike. **SCIENCE**: Robert H. Goddard suggests using rockets to reach the moon. ✳ Einstein's theory of relativity is supported by astronomical observations. **NEW PRODUCTS**: The Frigidaire refrigerator is introduced. **COMMUNICATION**: Dial telephones are introduced. **BUSINESS**: The Radio Corporation of America (RCA) is formed. ✳ Conrad Hilton starts a hotel business. **BOOKS**: *Ten Days That Shook the World* by John Reed, *Prejudices* by H.L. Mencken and *The Illiterate Digest* by Will Rogers. **MUSIC**: The Juilliard School of Music is founded. ✳ *A Pretty Girl Is Like a Melody*; *How 'Ya Gonna Keep 'Em Down on the Farm? (After They've Seen Pa-ree)*. **FILM**: *Male and Female* with Gloria Swanson; *The Cabinet of Dr. Caligari*; *The Sheik* with Rudolph Valentino; and the cartoon *Felix the Cat*. **FASHIONS**: Skirts suddenly rise to six inches above ground level. **SPORTS**: Thoroughbred Man o' War begins his racing career. ✳ The Cincinnati Reds defeat the Chicago White Sox to take the World Series. ✳ "Black Sox" scandal exposed. **FADS**: Ouija boards and pogo sticks are must-haves. **FAME**: Broadway stars include Al Jolson, Ann Pennington, Eddie Cantor, Will Rogers, W.C. Fields, Fanny Brice and Reginald Denny. **MISCELLANEOUS**: "Gasoline Alley" debuts in the *Chicago Tribune*.

1920

CATALOG *of Sources*

FAMILY
Milestones

HISTORICAL *Context of 1920*

HEADLINE: The 18th Amendment institutes the prohibition of alcohol in the U.S. Bootlegging becomes a big business. **GOVERNMENT**: Warren G. Harding and Calvin Coolidge elected President and VP. **TRAGEDY**: A bombing in front of the U.S. Sub-treasury on Wall Street. **CRIME**: Thousands of Bostonians are swindled in an investment fraud by Charles Ponzi. **CIVIL RIGHTS**: Marcus Garvey promotes a back-to-Africa movement. ✳ The American Civil Liberties Union is founded. ✳ The 19th Amendment gives women the vote. **LABOR**: The "Red scare" results in mass arrests of labor activists. **ORGANIZATIONS**: The League of Women Voters is founded. **RELIGION**: Evangelist "Billy" Sunday holds a mock funeral for "John Barleycorn." **NEW PRODUCTS**: Johnson & Johnson introduces Band-Aids. **FOOD**: The Baby Ruth candy bar and the Good Humor ice cream bar are introduced. **TRANSPORTATION**: Tetraethyl lead introduced to gasoline. **COMMUNICATION**: KDKA, in Pittsburgh, PA, becomes the first commercial radio station in U.S. **BOOKS**: *Main Street* by Sinclair Lewis, *The Age of Innocence* by Edith Wharton, *This Side of Paradise* by F. Scott Fitzgerald. **MUSIC**: *I'll Be With You in Apple Blossom Time* and *When My Baby Smiles at Me* are popular songs. **FILM**: *The Mark of Zorro* with Douglas Fairbanks; *The Kid* with Charlie Chaplin and Jackie Coogan. **FASHIONS**: Corsets are out of fashion. **SPORTS**: Formation of baseball's Negro National League. ✳ The Cleveland Indians defeat the Brooklyn Dodgers to take the World Series. ✳ Babe Ruth signs with the Yankees. **MISCELLANEOUS**: The first Miss America pageant at Atlantic City, NJ. **POPULATION**: U.S. population: 105,710,620. Urban population exceeds the rural.

1921

FAMILY Milestones

CATALOG *of Sources*

HEADLINE: Heart disease surpasses tuberculosis as the leading cause of death in America. **GOVERNMENT**: The U.S. General Accounting Office (GAO) is created. **MILITARY**: Brig. Gen. William Mitchell has a warship sunk to demonstrate air power. ✳ The U.S.S. Jupiter is converted into the first U.S. aircraft carrier. **CRIME**: The Ku Klux Klan spreads lawlessness in the South. **LABOR**: Labor activists Nicola Sacco and Bartolomeo Vanzetti are convicted of murder. **HEALTH**: Iodized salt is introduced. **SCIENCE**: Insulin is isolated. **NEW PRODUCTS**: Electrolux vacuum cleaners are introduced. **COMMUNICATION**: The first radio coverage of a World Series game by WJZ radio. **ECONOMICS**: Unemployment reaches 5.7 million. ✳ Overproduction causes farm prices to crash. **BUSINESS**: Armand Hammer begins his long trade relationship with the Soviet Union. **THEATER**: *Anna Christie* by Eugene O'Neil and *Shuffle Along* with Josephine Baker. **MUSIC**: *Blue Moon*; *I'm Just Wild About Harry*; *Secondhand Rose*; *California Here I Come*; *Ma! (He's Making Eyes at Me)*. **FASHIONS**: Hemlines rise to the knee. ✳ "Coco" Chanel introduces Chanel No. 5. ✳ Introduction of the Arrow shirt. **SPORTS**: Kenesaw Mountain Landis elected baseball commissioner. ✳ The New York Giants defeat the New York Yankees to take the World Series. **MISCELLANEOUS**: Americans raise $60 million to save Russians from famine. ✳ Benton MacKaye proposes a 2,000 mile Appalachian Trail for hikers. ✳ Creation of the slogan "I'd walk a mile for a Camel." ✳ Betty Crocker is created.

1922

CATALOG *of Sources*

FAMILY *Milestones*

HISTORICAL *Context of 1922*

HEADLINE: Oklahoma is placed under martial law to curb Ku Klux Klan activity. **CRIME**: The censorship of books in the U.S. creates a vast market for "Bookleggers." ✳ The Teapot Dome scandal is exposed. **CIVIL RIGHTS**: Rebecca L. Felton becomes the first woman U.S. Senator. **LABOR**: 26 men are killed when coal miners in Illinois riot. **SCIENCE**: Roy C. Andrews discovers fossil dinosaur eggs. ✳ E.V. McCollum treats rickets with vitamin D. **INVENTIONS**: The first successful Technicolor film process is developed. **BUSINESS**: Battle Creek Toasted Corn Flake Co. becomes the Kellogg Co. **BOOKS**: Novel *Babbitt* by Sinclair Lewis and poetry selections *The Waste Land* by T.S. Eliot, and *Harlem Shadows* by Claude McKay are published. ✳ *Etiquette—The Blue Book of Social Usage*, a book by Emily Post. **MAGAZINES**: *Better Homes and Gardens* and *Reader's Digest* begin publication. **THEATER**: *Abie's Irish Rose* by Anne Nichols. **MUSIC**: *Chicago; Rose of the Rio Grande; I'll See You in My Dreams; Way Down Yonder in New Orleans*. ✳ Louis Armstrong joins King Oliver's Creole Jazz Band. **FILM**: *Nanook of the North*, a documentary ✳ *Orphans of the Storm* with Lillian and Dorothy Gish. **SPORTS**: The New York Giants defeat The New York Yankees to take the World Series. ✳ Golfer Gene Sarazen takes the U.S. Open and PGA tournaments. ✳ Molla Mallory takes the U.S. Women's Open. **FADS**: The game mah-jongg is introduced. **FAME**: Charles Atlas named the "World's Most Perfectly Developed Man." **MISCELLANEOUS**: The first decentralized shopping center, Country Club Plaza Shopping Center, opens. ✳ A 20-ton meteor falls near Blackston, VA.

1923

CATALOG *of Sources*

FAMILY *Milestones*

HISTORICAL *Context of 1923*

HEADLINE: President Harding dies; Calvin Coolidge is sworn in. **LABOR**: U.S. Steel Corp. institutes an 8-hour workday. **ECOLOGY**: A cloud of grasshoppers 300 miles (480 km) long, 100 miles (160 km) wide, and half a mile (.8 km) high devastates Montana. **INVENTIONS**: The bulldozer is invented. **NEW PRODUCTS**: First electric shaver by Col. Jacob Schick. **FOOD**: Curtiss Candy Co. introduces Butterfinger candy bar. **ECONOMICS**: Intermediate Credits Act expands credit to farmers. **BUSINESS**: John D. Hertz founds the Hertz Drive-Ur-Self System. ✳ Arthur Charles Nielsen founds the A.C. Nielsen Co. **BOOKS**: Poetry collections include *Stopping by Woods on a Snowy Evening* by Robert Frost; *The Prophet*, by Kahlil Gibran. **MAGAZINES**: *Time* begins publication. **MUSIC**: Violinist Yehudi Menuhin makes his public debut at age seven. ✳ The Boogie Woogie music style is hot. ✳ *Yes, We Have No Bananas*; *It Ain't Gonna Rain No Mo'*; *Down-Hearted Blues*; *Sonny Boy*; *Tea for Two*. **DANCES**: The Charleston and the first dance marathons are popularized. **FILM**: *The Ten Commandments* by Cecil B. DeMille and *Safety Last* with Harold Lloyd. **SPORTS**: Bill Tilden takes the men's singles in the U.S. Open. ✳ The New York Yankees defeat the New York Giants to take World Series. **FADS**: "Day by day in every way I am getting better and better:" magical words to heal you by "miracle healer" Emile Coue. **OCCASIONS**: President Coolidge starts a tradition by lighting the first White House Christmas tree. **MISCELLANEOUS**: The cartoon strip "Moon Mullins" is launched.

1924

CATALOG *of Sources*

FAMILY
Milestones

HISTORICAL *Context of 1924*

HEADLINE: Numerous gangland murders in Chicago connected to liquor trafficking. **GOVERNMENT**: Calvin Coolidge and Charles Dawes elected President and VP. **CRIME**: Rev. Warren K. Robinson is arrested for violating the Mann Act. ✳ J. Edgar Hoover heads the Bureau of Investigation. ✳ Nathan Leopold and Richard Loeb, both 19, confess murdering cousin "Bobby" Franks. **CIVIL RIGHTS**: The Bursum Bill, to allow squatters on Pueblo Indian lands, is defeated. ✳ Native-born Indians are granted full citizenship. **HEALTH**: George and Gladys Dick isolate scarlet fever streptococcus. **SCIENCE**: Edwin Hubble proves existence of other galaxies. **INVENTIONS**: Kodak introduces cellulose acetate film. **NEW PRODUCTS**: Introduction of *Celluwipes*, (renamed *Kleenex*.) **TRANSPORTATION**: Diesel electric locomotives go into service. ✳ Two World Cruisers circumnavigate the globe. **ECONOMICS**: Owens Valley farmers blow up Los Angeles city water gates. **BUSINESS**: IBM is organized. **BOOKS**: *So Big* a novel by Edna Ferber. **THEATER**: *All God's Chillun Got Wings*, a play. **MUSIC**: *Sweet Georgia Brown*; *It Had to Be You*; *Rhapsody in Blue*. **FILM**: *Greed* by Eric von Stroheim; *The Navigator* with Buster Keaton. **SPORTS**: Notre Dame fields "The Four Horsemen of the Apocalypse." ✳ The Washington Senators defeat the New York Giants to take the World Series. ✳ U.S. athletes shine at the first Winter Olympics. **OCCASIONS**: The first Macy's Thanksgiving Day Parade. **NOTORIETY**: Trinity College changes its name to Duke University for $47 million. **FAME**: "Shipwreck Kelly" starts the flagpole sitting craze. **MISCELLANEOUS**: The comic strip "Little Orphan Annie" debuts.

1925

FAMILY
Milestones

HEADLINE: In an investigative article, *Collier's* becomes the first major magazine to call for a repeal of Prohibition. **CRIME**: Al Capone takes over as boss of Chicago bootleggers. ✳ Florida land values take a tumble when many discover their properties are underwater. **LABOR**: *The Autobiography of Mother Jones* by union organizer Mary Harris Jones. **EDUCATION**: Tennessee tries John Scopes for teaching evolution. ✳ National Spelling Bee begun. **HEALTH**: Prominent medical associations endorse birth control. **ORGANIZATIONS**: The John Simon Guggenheim Memorial Foundation is established. **NEW PRODUCTS**: Clarence Birdseye markets quick-frozen foods. ✳ Electric percolators are introduced. **TRANSPORTATION**: The *20th Century Limited* has a mile-a-minute schedule from New York to Chicago. ✳ James Vail opens America's first motel in San Luis Obispo, CA. **COMMUNICATION**: Radio WSM in Nashville, TN, airs *WSM Barn Dance (The Grand Ole Opry)*. **BUSINESS**: Automaker Walter P. Chrysler founds the Chrysler Corporation. **BOOKS**: Novels include *Arrowsmith* by Sinclair Lewis and *Gentlemen Prefer Blondes* by Anita Loos. **MAGAZINES**: *The New Yorker* begins publication. **THEATER**: *The Cocoanuts* a musical with the Four Marx Brothers and Margaret Dumont. **MUSIC**: *Five Feet Two, Eyes of Blue*; *I Dreamed I Saw Joe Hill Last Night*; *Yes, Sir, That's My Baby*. **FILM**: *The Gold Rush* with Charlie Chaplin; *The Eagle* with Rudolph Valentino. **SPORTS**: The Pittsburgh Pirates defeat the Washington Senators to take the World Series. ✳ Helen Wills takes the U.S. Open Women's Singles. ✳ Lou Gehrig joins the Yankees. **MISCELLANEOUS**: 40,000 march in Ku Klux Klan rally in Washington, DC. ✳ Lucky Strike and Chesterfield ads encourage women to smoke.

1926

FAMILY
Milestones

CATALOG *of Sources*

HISTORICAL *Context of 1926*

HEADLINE: Eight touring cars in single file spray machine gun fire at Al Capone's headquarters. **CRIME**: Prohibition laws have created a $3.6 billion illegal liquor business. **LABOR**: Ford announces 8 hour day, 5 day work week. **EDUCATION**: Museum of Science and Industry opens in Chicago. **RELIGION**: Jiddu Krishnamurti comes to America proclaiming the Second Coming of Christ. **EXPLORATION**: Richard E. Byrd and pilot Floyd Bennett fly over the north pole. **SCIENCE**: The speed of light is accurately measured. ✳ Robert Goddard launches his first liquid fueled rocket. **NEW PRODUCTS**: Slide fasteners are christened "zippers." **TRANSPORTATION**: The Air Commerce Act creates the federal airway system. ✳ Safety glass windshields make their debut. **BUSINESS**: David Sarnoff founds NBC. **BOOKS**: *Showboat*, a novel by Edna Ferber; *The Weary Blues*, poetry by Langston Hughes; and a children's book *The Little Engine That Could* by Watty Piper are published. **ART**: *Black Iris*, a painting by Georgia O'Keeffe. **MUSIC**: *Bye Bye Blackbird*; *Smoke House Blues*; *Doctor Jazz*; *Blue Skies* and *Baby Face*. **FILM**: *The General* with Buster Keaton; *Son of the Sheik* with Rudolph Valentino. **SPORTS**: Gene Tunney beats Jack Dempsey for the heavyweight title. ✳ The St. Louis Cardinals defeat the New York Yankees to take the World Series. ✳ Gertrude Ederle is the first woman to swim the English Channel. ✳ Frieda Carter invents miniature golf ✳ The Harlem Globetrotters basketball team is organized in Chicago. **NOTORIETY**: Evangelist Aimee Semple McPherson kidnapping hoax and scandal. ✳ Father Coughlin begins his infamous radio career. **FAME**: Tens of thousands mourn Rudolph Valentino at Campbell's Funeral Church. **MISCELLANEOUS**: Book-of-the-Month Club begins.

1927

FAMILY
Milestones

CATALOG *of Sources*

HEADLINE: Charles Lindbergh solos in the *Spirit of St. Louis* from New York to Paris. **TRAGEDY**: Over 300 people die in flooding along the Mississippi River. ✳ Isadora Duncan is killed in a car accident. **LABOR**: Sacco and Vanzetti die in the electric chair despite international appeals. **ORGANIZATIONS**: Louis B. Mayer founds the Academy of Motion Picture Arts and Sciences. **SCIENCE**: A spearhead is found in an Ice Age bison skeleton near Folsom, NM. **FOOD**: Introduction of Wonder Bread, Hostess Cakes, homogenized milk, and the "monitor top" refrigerator. **TRANSPORTATION**: After 15 million Model Ts, Ford introduces the Model A. ✳ Telephone service begins between London and New York. **BOOKS**: *Elmer Gantry* by Upton Sinclair and *Death Comes for the Archbishop* by Willa Cather are published. **THEATER**: The muscial *Show Boat* opens for a run through the thirties. **MUSIC**: Duke Ellington's jazz band stars at Harlem's *Cotton Club* in New York City. ✳ *Old Man River*; *Let a Smile Be Your Umbrella*; *Blue Skies*; *Ain't She Sweet*; *I'm Looking Over a Four Leaf Clover*. ✳ Introduction of the all-electric jukebox. **DANCES**: The varsity drag is in. ✳ Martha Graham opens a dance studio in New York City. **FILM**: *The Jazz Singer* with Al Jolson; *Flesh and the Devil* with Greta Garbo. **FASHIONS**: Women's hemlines rise above the knee. **SPORTS**: Babe Ruth hits his 60th homer in 154 games. ✳ The New York Yankees defeat the Pittsburgh Pirates to take the World Series. ✳ First Golden Gloves amateur boxing matches. **MISCELLANEOUS**: Mount Rushmore, SD, is dedicated.

1928

FAMILY
Milestones

HEADLINE: Prohibition toll: 1,500 dead, hundreds blinded from bad liquor, and dozens killed in shootings. **GOVERNMENT**: Herbert Hoover and Charles Curtis elected president and VP. **TRAGEDY**: 350 perish when the St. Francis Dam in California bursts. **CIVIL RIGHTS**: The Meriam Report reveals gross abuses within the Bureau of Indian Affairs. **ORGANIZATIONS**: The National Conference of Christians and Jews is founded. **INVENTIONS**: The first quartz clock is built. **FOOD**: Introduction of Kellogg's Rice Krispies, Peter Pan peanut butter and Fleer's bubble gum. **TRANSPORTATION**: The Tamiami Trail across Florida opens. **COMMUNICATION**: WGY in Schenectady, NY broadcasts the first regularly scheduled television programs. ✳ *Amos 'n' Andy* premieres on WMAQ in Chicago. **ECONOMICS**: Boeing Company is founded. **BOOKS**: *Coming of Age in Samoa* by Margaret Mead is published. **MUSIC**: *Sweet Lorraine*; *Stout-Hearted Men*; *Button Up Your Overcoat*; *Lover, Come Back to Me*; *American in Paris*; *Puttin' on the Ritz*; *You're the Cream in My Coffee*. ✳ Lawrence Welk starts a band in South Dakota. ✳ Arturo Toscanini becomes conductor of the New York Philharmonic. **FILM**: *Steamboat Willie* with Mickey Mouse. **SPORTS**: Ty Cobb retires with a lifetime batting record of .367. ✳ The New York Yankees defeat the St. Louis Cardinals to take the World Series. **FADS**: A dance marathon in Madison Square Garden runs for 481 hours before being shut down by the board of health. **FAME**: Crooner Rudy Vallée debuts. ✳ Amelia Earhart becomes the first woman to solo across the Atlantic. **MISCELLANEOUS**: Bryce Canyon National Park is created.

1929

CATALOG *of Sources*

FAMILY
Milestones

HISTORICAL *Context of 1929*

HEADLINE: On "Black Tuesday," the Dow Jones plummets from 381 to 31, and a worldwide depression begins. **GOVERNMENT**: Hoover appoints commission to study effects of Prohibition on the U.S. **CRIME**: Members of the "Bugs" Moran gang are machine-gunned in the St. Valentine's Day Massacre. **HEALTH**: 30 percent of children surveyed in Baltimore have rickets. ✷ The link between hypertension and heart disease is demonstrated. **ORGANIZATIONS**: The Workers Party of America is renamed the Communist Party of the United States. ✷ Dallas teachers form the first Blue Cross health insurance group. ✷ Seeing Eye is founded to provide guide dogs for the blind. **EXPLORATION**: Richard E. Byrd flies over the South Pole. **SCIENCE**: Edwin Hubble proves the universe is expanding by measuring the "red shift." **NEW PRODUCTS**: Radburn, NJ, is the site of a prototype "Garden Community." **FOOD**: 7UP is introduced as Lithiated Lemon. **TRANSPORTATION**: First air-conditioned passenger rail cars. **BOOKS**: *The Sound and the Fury* by William Faulkner, *The Roman Hat Mystery* by Ellery Queen and *Red Harvest* by Dashiell Hammett are published. **ART**: The Museum of Modern Art opens in New York City. **MUSIC**: *Tiptoe Though the Tulips*; *With a Song in My Heart*; *Ain't Misbehavin'*; *I'm Just a Vagabond Lover*; *Happy Days Are Here Again*. **FILM**: *The Broadway Melody*, a "backstage" musical. **SPORTS**: A recruiting scandal in college football. ✷ The Philadelphia Athletics defeat the Chicago Cubs to take the World Series. **FADS**: The pinball machine and yo-yo are introduced. **OCCASIONS**: The first Academy Awards. **MISCELLANEOUS**: Debut of Popeye character in "Thimble Theatre."

1930

CATALOG *of Sources*

FAMILY *Milestones*

HISTORICAL *Context of 1930*

HEADLINE: 4.5 million unemployed. More than 1,300 banks go belly up. **GOVERNMENT**: Congress establishes the Veterans Administration. ✳ Annual farm income is $400 per family, many are subsistence farmers. **RELIGION**: The American Lutheran Church formed. **ECOLOGY**: Dutch elm disease breaks out in Ohio. **SCIENCE**: Annie Cannon retires after cataloging more than 400,000 astronomical objects. ✳ Planet Pluto is discovered. ✳ The human egg cell is viewed through a microscope for the first time. **INVENTIONS**: The first analog computer is developed by Vannevar Bush. **FOOD**: Introduction of Twinkies and Snickers. **TRANSPORTATION**: United Airlines hires the first airline stewardesses. **BOOKS**: *The Maltese Falcon*, by Dashiell Hammett, introduces the character Sam Spade; *Bring 'Em Back Alive* by Frank Buck; *Hitty, Her First Hundred Years* by Rachel Field. **THEATER**: *Girl Crazy* with Ethel Merman. **ART**: *American Gothic*, a painting by Grant Wood; *Early Sunday Morning* by Edward Hopper. **MUSIC**: *Little White Lies*; *Dream a Little Dream of Me*; *Georgia on My Mind*; *I Got Rhythm*; *Body and Soul*. **RADIO**: *Death Valley Days*. **FILM**: *Anna Christie* with Greta Garbo; *The Big Trail* with John Wayne; *All Quiet on the Western Front*; *Animal Crackers* with the Marx Brothers. **SPORTS**: Bobby Jones takes the U.S. Open Golf Championship. ✳ The Philadelphia Athletics defeat the St. Louis Cardinals to take the World Series. **FADS**: Irish Sweepstakes established. **NOTORIETY**: Helen Morgan creates a sensation singing *My Man* while perched on the piano in a sultry manner. **MISCELLANEOUS**: The comic strip "Blondie" by Chic Young debuts in Chicago. **POPULATION**: U.S. population 122,775,046.

1931

CATALOG *of Sources*

FAMILY *Milestones*

HEADLINE: 2,300 banks fail; panic spreads. Unemployment tops 8 million. **TRAGEDY**: 20,000 persons commit suicide in 1931. **CRIME**: Al Capone is jailed for income tax evasion. ✳ President Hoover's Wichersham Committee reports that Prohibition is not working. **LABOR**: Coal miners and private guards shoot it out in Harlan County, KY. **RELIGION**: Jehovah's Witnesses founded. **EXPLORATION**: Wiley Post and Harold Gatty fly *Winnie Mae* around the world in less than 9 days. **SCIENCE**: J.G. Lansky discovers radio waves from outer space. ✳ Heavy water is discovered by physicists at Columbia University. **INVENTIONS**: Fiberglass and neoprene rubber are introduced. ✳ Nylon is invented by W.H. Carothers. **NEW PRODUCTS**: Alka-Seltzer and Clairol hair dye are introduced. **ECONOMICS**: A record wheat crop depresses prices. **BUSINESS**: Potash from New Mexico mines make the U.S. self-sufficient in fertilizer. **BOOKS**: *The Good Earth* by Pearl S. Buck and *Guys and Dolls* by Damon Runyon. **MUSIC**: *That Silver-Haired Daddy of Mine*; *Mood Indigo*; *All of Me*; *I Love a Parade*. **RADIO**: Popular new shows: *The Easy Aces*; *Little Orphan Annie*. ✳ Kate Smith begins her radio career. **FILM**: *Frankenstein* with Boris Karloff; *Dracula* with Bela Lugosi; *Platinum Blond* with Jean Harlow. **SPORTS**: The St. Louis Cardinals defeat the Philadelphia Athletics to take the World Series. **FADS**: Fortean Society is founded to ridicule science. **OCCASIONS**: *The Star Spangled Banner* becomes the national anthem. **MISCELLANEOUS**: The *Chicago Tribune* introduces the comic strip "Dick Tracy." ✳ Empire State Building dedicated. ✳ Nevada legalizes gambling.

1932

CATALOG *of Sources*

FAMILY *Milestones*

HEADLINE: Franklin D. Roosevelt and John N. Garner elected president and VP. **GOVERNMENT**: Congress releases 85 million bushels of wheat to feed starving Americans. **MILITARY**: MacArthur, Eisenhower and Patton lead tanks, cavalry and infantry to disperse "Bonus Marchers," and their wives and children from Washington. **CRIME**: The Lindbergh baby is kidnapped. **LABOR**: Dearborn, MI, police fire into a crowd of demonstrators outside the Ford Motor Co. plant. **SCIENCE**: Ernest Orlando Lawrence builds the world's first cyclotron. ✳ Dr Charles Glen King isolates vitamin C. **NEW PRODUCTS**: Zippo manufacturing introduces the Zippo lighter. **FOOD**: Introduction of the 3 Musketeers bar and Skippy peanut butter. **TRANSPORTATION**: Route 66 opens between Chicago and Los Angeles. **ECONOMICS**: Between 13 and 17 million are unemployed. **BUSINESS**: Revlon is founded. **BOOKS**: *Tobacco Road* by Erskine Caldwell and *Little House in the Big Woods* by Laura Ingalls Wilder. **THEATER**: Radio City Music Hall opens in New York City's Rockefeller Center. **ART**: Sculptor Alexander Calder creates his first mobile. **MUSIC**: *Grand Canyon Suite*, a symphony by Ferde Grofe. ✳ *Let's Have Another Cup of Coffee*; *Brother, Can You Spare a Dime*; *Night and Day*. **RADIO**: *The Walter Winchell Show, Buck Rogers in the Twenty-Fifth Century* and *The Jack Benny Show* are favorites. **FILM**: *Tarzan, The Ape Man* with Johnny Weismuller; *The Big Broadcast* with Kate Smith, the Mills Brothers, Cab Calloway and Bing Crosby. **SPORTS**: Lake Placid, NY, hosts the Winter Olympic Games. ✳ The New York Yankees defeat the Chicago Cubs to take the World Series.

1933

CATALOG *of Sources*

FAMILY
Milestones

HISTORICAL *Context of 1933*

HEADLINE: The 21st Amendment repeals Prohibition. **GOVERNMENT**: Roosevelt launches programs to get the U.S. out of the depression: NRA, PWA, NIRA, CCC, Emergency Banking Act and Federal Securities Act. ✳ U.S. abandons the gold standard. **HEALTH**: Sodium Pentothal used for anesthesia. **ECOLOGY**: The first year of the "Dust Bowl." **INVENTIONS**: Edwin Armstrong invents frequency modulation (FM). **FOOD**: Introduction of Ritz Crackers and vitamin-D fortified Borden milk. **MAGAZINES**: *Esquire* and *Newsweek* begin publication. **ART**: Mexican artist Diego Rivera's mural at the Rockefeller Center is destroyed. **MUSIC**: *Basin Street Blues*; *Sophisticated Lady*; *Minnie the Moocher*; *We're in the Money*; *Easter Parade*; *Heat Wave*. **DANCE**: Kirstein and Balanchine found the *School of American Ballet*. **RADIO**: Roosevelt begins his fireside chats; *The Lone Ranger* debuts. **FILM**: *She Done Him Wrong* with Mae West, *King Kong* and *International House* with W.C. Fields. **FASHIONS**: Helen Jacobs wears shorts in tennis tournaments. **SPORTS**: Chicago Bears beat the New York Giants in the first NFL championship. ✳ The American League defeats the National League in the first All-Star game. ✳ The New York Giants defeat the Washington Senators to take the World Series. **FADS**: The speakeasies of the Prohibition era become cafes or chic restaurants. ✳ The Dy-Dee-Doll drinks water from a bottle and wets its diaper. **OCCASIONS**: Century of Progress Exhibition in Chicago. **FAME**: "Poor little rich girl" Barbara Hutton marries Prince Mdivani in Paris. ✳ Albert Einstein arrives in the U.S. ✳ Sally Rand does the fan dance at Chicago World's Fair. **MISCELLANEOUS**: The Budweiser Clydesdale horses appear the day after Prohibiton is ended.

1934

FAMILY Milestones

CATALOG of Sources

HISTORICAL *Context of 1934*

HEADLINE: Bonnie Parker and Clyde Barrow, "Pretty Boy" Floyd and John Dillinger are killed by law officers. **CIVIL RIGHTS**: The Indian Reorganization Act reverses the allotment policy. **LABOR**: The National Labor Relations Board is created. **ORGANIZATIONS**: The Liberty League is founded to oppose New Deal economic measures. **RELIGION**: Elijah Muhammad becomes leader of the Nation of Islam. **ECOLOGY**: *A Field Guide to the Birds* by Roger Tory Peterson. ✷ The Taylor Grazing Act is passed by Congress. **INVENTIONS**: First pipeless Hammond organ. **TRANSPORTATION**: American Airlines introduces travel by credit card. **ECONOMICS**: Gold Reserve Act. ✷ Joseph P. Kennedy becomes head of the newly created Securities and Exchange Commission. **BUSINESS**: J.F. Cantrell opens the first laundromat in Fort Worth, TX. ✷ Muzak Corporation is founded. **BOOKS**: *Tropic of Cancer*, a novel by Henry Miller; *Goodbye, Mr. Chips* by James Hilton. **THEATER**: *The Children's Hour* by Lillian Hellman; *Anything Goes* with score by Cole Porter. **MUSIC**: *On the Good Ship Lollipop*; *Winter Wonderland*; *Tumbling Tumbleweeds*. **FILM**: *Babes in Toyland* with Laurel and Hardy; *Little Miss Marker* with Shirley Temple. ✷ The Catholic Legion of Decency begins censoring movies. **SPORTS**: The football is standardized. ✷ The St. Louis Cardinals defeat the Detroit Tigers to take the World Series. **FAME**: Shirley Temple's success in the movies spurs a merchandizing frenzy. ✷ Successful birth of the Dionne Quintuplets. **MISCELLANEOUS**: "Li'l Abner" and "Flash Gordon" cartoon strips make their debut. ✷ Great Smoky Mountains National Park is created. **POPULATION**: "Okies," not all of them from Oklahoma, migrate west to escape the Dust Bowl.

1935

CATALOG *of Sources*

FAMILY
Milestones

HEADLINE: The Wagner Act forces employers to accept collective bargaining. **GOVERNMENT**: Rural Electrification Administration established. ✳ The Social Security Act is signed into law. ✳ The Works Progress Administration (WPA) is created. ✳ The Soil Conservation Act is signed into law. **CRIME**: Louisiana governor Huey Long is shot and killed. ✳ Feds kill Fred and "Ma" Barker outside of Ocklawaha, FL. **LABOR**: United Automobile Workers (UAW) is founded. ✳ Committee for Industrial Organization (CIO) established. **ORGANIZATIONS**: Alcoholics Anonymous is founded in New York. **SCIENCE**: Uranium-235 is discovered. **INVENTIONS**: Gibson Guitar Co. invents the electric guitar. **FOOD**: Krueger Beer is the first canned beer in the U.S. **BOOKS**: *Tortilla Flat*, a novel by John Steinbeck. **THEATER**: *Porgy and Bess* by George and Ira Gershwin. **MUSIC**: *I Got Plenty o' Nuttin*; *Red Sails in the Sunset*; *Moon Over Miami*; *I'm in the Mood for Love*. **DANCES**: Benny Goodman introduces his "big band" jazz music on the radio program *Let's Dance*. **RADIO**: A popular program is *Fibber McGee and Molly*. **FILM**: *Top Hat* with Fred Astaire and Ginger Rogers; *Captain Blood* with Errol Flynn and Olivia de Havilland. **SPORTS**: The Detroit Tigers defeat the Chicago Cubs to take the World Series. ✳ The first major league night baseball game. ✳ Jay Berwanger is the first Heisman Trophy winner. **FADS**: Parker Brothers introduces *Monopoly*. ✳ The chain-letter craze begins in Denver, CO. **NOTORIETY**: *Clashing Tides of Color* by Lothrop Stoddard claims that the superior "white race" is being diluted and overrun by inferior races. **FAME**: Mae West earns second largest salary in U.S.

1936

CATALOG *of Sources*

FAMILY
Milestones

HISTORICAL *Context of 1936*

HEADLINE: Franklin D. Roosevelt and John Garner are reelected president and VP. **LABOR**: Sit-down strikes spread across the nation. GM accepts the UAW as the bargaining agent for striking workers. **HEALTH**: Vitamin E is isolated. **ORGANIZATIONS**: Father Charles Coughlin and others form the Union for Social Justice Party. **ECOLOGY**: The Soil Conservation and Domestic Allotment Act is passed. **INVENTIONS**: Introduction of 35mm Kodachrome film and the Waring blender. **TRANSPORTATION**: Douglas Aircraft introduces the DC-3. **ECONOMICS**: One-third of Americans live below the poverty level. ✳ Catalytic cracking (a process that increased gasoline production) lowers gas prices. **BOOKS**: *How to Win Friends and Influence People* by Dale Carnegie; *Gone With the Wind* by Margaret Mitchell; *The Last Puritan* by George Santayana; *The Joy of Cooking* by Irma S. Rombauer. **MAGAZINES**: *Life* magazine is launched. **MUSIC**: *Pennies from Heaven*; *Walking Blues*; *Cool Water*; *I'm an Old Cowhand from the Rio Grande*. **RADIO**: *The Shadow, Lux Radio Theatre*. **FILM**: *Three Smart Girls* with Deanna Durbin; *Fury* with Spencer Tracy; *Modern Times* with Charlie Chaplin. **SPORTS**: The National Baseball Hall of Fame opens in Cooperstown, NY. ✳ Max Schmeling defeats Joe Louis. ✳ Jesse Owens wins four gold medals at Berlin Olympics. ✳ The New York Yankees defeat the New York Giants to take the World Series. ✳ Alice Marble wins the women's U.S. Open in Tennis. **FADS**: Jive talk includes the words "alligator, canary, hepcat, in the groove, long hair." **NOTORIETY**: Bruno Hauptmann is executed for the murder of the Lindbergh baby. **MISCELLANEOUS**: Boulder Dam is completed in Arizona.

1937

CATALOG *of Sources*

FAMILY
Milestones

HEADLINE: The airship *Hindenburg* explodes upon her arrival in Lakehurst, NJ. **GOVERNMENT**: Roosevelt tries to pack the Supreme Court. ✳ The Marijuana Traffic Act outlaws possession and sale of marijuana. **TRAGEDY**: 294 students die in a natural gas explosion in New London, TX. ✳ 500,000 are left homeless when the Ohio River floods. ✳ Amelia Earhart disappears while on a flight around the world. **LABOR**: United Steel Workers Union is accepted as the union bargaining agent by steel companies. **RELIGION**: Faithful Mary, Father Divine's Angel Number 1, denounces him as a hypocrite and fraud. **NEW PRODUCTS**: Spam and shopping carts are introduced. ✳ *Sellotape*, cellophane tape, is introduced. **TRANSPORTATION**: GM introduces an automatic transmission for cars. **BUSINESS**: Howard Johnson restaurants are founded. **BOOKS**: *Of Mice and Men* by John Steinbeck; *Noon Wine* by Katherine Anne Porter. **MAGAZINES**: *Look* and *Newsweek* magazines begin publication. **MUSIC**: *Harbor Lights*; *It Looks Like Rain*; *Sweet Leilani*; *Thanks for the Memory*; *Bei MirBist Du Schön (Means I Love You)*; *Blue Hawaii*. **RADIO**: *The Guiding Light*; *The Charlie McCarthy Show*. **FILM**: *A Day at the Races* with the Marx Brothers, *Way Out West* with Laurel and Hardy; *A Star Is Born* with Fredric March and Janet Gaynor; *Topper* with Cary Grant and Constance Bennett. **FASHIONS**: Panama hats are fashionable for men. **SPORTS**: The New York Yankees defeat the New York Giants to take the World Series. ✳ The National Basketball League is founded. **FAME**: Margarita Carmen Cansino changes her name to Rita Hayworth. **MISCELLANEOUS**: The Golden Gate Bridge is dedicated.

1938

FAMILY
Milestones

CATALOG *of Sources*

HEADLINE: A onetime science fiction special, *The War of the Worlds*, by Orson Welles, causes widespread hysteria in many cities. **GOVERNMENT**: Congress passes a Flood Control Act authorizing public works projects. ✷ Establishment of the House Committee on Un-American Activities. **LABOR**: The Congress of Industrial Organizations is organized. ✷ Fair Labor Standards Law sets minimum wages at $.25 per hour. **ORGANIZATIONS**: The March of Dimes is founded. **SCIENCE**: Teflon is discovered. **INVENTIONS**: The self-propelled combine is introduced. ✷ Chester Carlson invents xerography. **NEW PRODUCTS**: Nylon toothbrushes go on sale. **ECONOMICS**: Unemployment reaches 19 percent. **BUSINESS**: Drive-in banking is introduced at City National Bank of South Bend, IN. **BOOKS**: *Northwest Passage* by Kenneth Roberts; *Mei Li* by Thomas Handforth. **THEATER**: *Our Town*, a play by Thornton Wilder. **MUSIC**: *A-Tisket, A-Tasket*; *Jeepers Creepers*; *Whistle While You Work*; *You Must Have Been a Beautiful Baby*; *My Reverie*. ✷ *Adagio for Strings* by Samuel Barber. ✷ Glenn Miller forms his band. ✷ "Canary" Billie Holiday joins Artie Shaw's Orchestra. **DANCES**: The Samba and the Conga are introduced. **RADIO**: *The Green Hornet* is a popular show. **FILM**: *Boys' Town* with Spencer Tracy; *Holiday* with Katharine Hepburn and Cary Grant; *Love Finds Andy Hardy* with Mickey Rooney; *Snow White and the Seven Dwarfs* by Walt Disney. **FASHIONS**: Brenda Frazier sets the fashion trend with a strapless evening gown. **SPORTS**: Bob Feller strikes out 18 batters in a single game. ✷ The New York Yankees defeat the Chicago Cubs to take the World Series. **MISCELLANEOUS**: "Wrong-Way Corrigan" flies to Dublin, Ireland instead of California. ✷ *Superman* character debuts in *Action Comics*.

1939

FAMILY Milestones

CATALOG of Sources

HISTORICAL *Context of 1939*

HEADLINE: Having been denied access to Washington's Constitution Hall because of her race, Marian Anderson gives a concert for over 75,000 people at the Lincoln Memorial on Easter Sunday. **GOVERNMENT**: Congress passes the Hatch Act. **ORGANIZATIONS**: The United Jewish Appeal is founded. **SCIENCE**: Albert Einstein sends a letter to Roosevelt explaining the potential of an atomic bomb. ✳ The uranium atom is split. **FOOD**: Precooked frozen foods are introduced. **TRANSPORTATION**: Pan Am introduces transatlantic air travel. **BOOKS**: *The Grapes of Wrath*, by John Steinbeck; "The Secret Life of Walter Mitty," a short story by James Thurber. ✳ Paperbacks go on sale. **ART**: Edward Chavez completes the mural *The Pioneers*. **MUSIC**: *God Bless America*; *Body and Soul*; *Beer Barrel Polka*; *Sunrise Serenade*; *In the Mood*. ✳ Band leaders include Benny Goodman, Artie Shaw, Tommy Dorsey, Glenn Miller, Count Basie, Jimmy Dorsey, Harry James and Duke Ellington. **RADIO**: *Young Doctor Malone*; *Lil' Abner*. ✳ IBC is established to produce Spanish language radio programming. **FILM**: *The Wizard of Oz* with Judy Garland; *Gone With the Wind* with Clark Gable, Vivien Leigh; *The Hunchback of Notre Dame*, with Charles Laughton and Maureen O'Hara; *Destry Rides Again* with Gary Cooper. **TV**: The first broadcast of a baseball game. **FASHIONS**: Bare midriffs are popular in summer. ✳ Nylon stockings go on sale. **SPORTS**: Lou Gehrig retires after 2,130 consecutive games. ✳ The New York Yankees defeat the Cincinnati Reds to take the World Series. ✳ Formation of Little League baseball. **FADS**: Goldfish swallowing on college campuses. **MISCELLANEOUS**: Jewish refugees aboard the *S.S. St. Louis* are denied entry into the U.S. ✳ Batman debuts in *Detective Comics* ✳ Bugs Bunny cartoons debut.

1940

CATALOG *of Sources*

FAMILY *Milestones*

HISTORICAL *Context of 1940*

HEADLINE: The first peacetime draft goes into effect. **GOVERNMENT**: FDR and Henry Wallace elected president and VP. **MILITARY**: The U.S. Signal Corps cracks Japan's top diplomatic code. **CIVIL RIGHTS**: Charles R. Drew opens the first blood bank, but he is not allowed to donate because of segregation laws. **LABOR**: 40-hour workweek goes into effect. **HEALTH**: Eleanor Roosevelt endorses birth control. **SCIENCE**: The invention of the electron microscope. **FOOD**: Mars develops *M&M*s for GIs. **TRANSPORTATION**: The first U.S. superhighway, the Pennsylvania Turnpike, opens. **BOOKS**: *The Heart Is a Lonely Hunter* by Carson McCullers; *For Whom the Bell Tolls* by Ernest Hemingway; *Native Son* by Richard Wright. **MAGAZINES**: *Billboard* magazine is launched. **MUSIC**: *You Are my Sunshine*; *When You Wish Upon a Star*; *Blueberry Hill*; *Beat Me, Daddy, Eight to the Bar*; *San Antonio Rose*. **DANCE**: The Lindy Hop. **RADIO**: Edward R. Murrow begins broadcasting from London. ✳ Popular radio shows include *Gangbusters*, *Fibber McGee and Molly* and *The Jack Benny Show*. **FILM**: *Fantasia* by Walt Disney; *The Bank Dick* with W.C. Fields; *His Girl Friday* with Cary Grant and Rosiland Russell; *The Grapes of Wrath*, with Henry Fonda and Jane Darwell; *Road to Singapore* with Bing Crosby, Bob Hope and Dorothy Lamour. **SPORTS**: The Cincinnati Reds defeat the Detroit Tigers to take the World Series. **FADS**: The Zoot suit. **NOTORIETY**: Wilhelm Reich builds his orgone energy accumulator to concentrate a special energy to cure human ills. **POPULATION**: U.S. population 131,669,275 ✳ 528,431 immigrants entered the U.S in the previous decade.

1941

CATALOG *of Sources*

FAMILY
Milestones

HEADLINE: Japan attacks Pearl Harbor, HI; America enters WWII. **GOVERNMENT**: President Roosevelt talks of Four Freedoms in his State of the Union speech. **MILITARY**: Roosevelt and Churchill agree on an Atlantic Charter. ✳ Leslie Groves heads the Manhattan Project to develop an atomic bomb. ✳ "Rosie the Riveter" popularizes the American woman's role in defense industries. ✳ "Sad Sack" appears in military papers. **CIVIL RIGHTS**: Racial discrimination is outlawed in the defense industry. **ORGANIZATIONS**: Isolationists unite under the America First Committee. **SCIENCE**: Plutonium is isolated. **FOOD**: General Mills introduces Cheerios. **TRANSPORTATION**: Diesel freight locomotives go into service. **ECONOMICS**: Unemployment is 10 percent. **BOOKS**: *Curious George* by H.A. Rey and Margaret Rey; *Make Way for Ducklings*, by Robert McCloskey. **THEATER**: *Arsenic and Old Lace* by Joseph Kesselring. **ART**: *Nighthawks*, a painting by Edward Hopper. ✳ The National Gallery of Art is dedicated. **MUSIC**: *We Did It Before (And We Can Do It Again)*; *Deep in the Heart of Texas*; *Chattanooga Choo-Choo*; *Orange Blossom Special*; *Boogie Woogie Bugle Boy*. **RADIO**: *The Red Skelton Show*; *The Thin Man*. **FILM**: *Citizen Kane* by Orson Welles; *The Maltese Falcon* with Humphrey Bogart; *The Wolf Man* with Lon Chaney, Jr.; *Buck Privates* with Abbott and Costello. ✳ Greta Garbo retires from public life. **FASHIONS**: Short skirts become fashionable as government regulations limit the amount of fabric available. ✳ Veronica Lake starts a hairstyle craze with a "peek-a-boo" look. **SPORTS**: Whirlaway takes the Triple Crown. ✳ Joe DiMaggio hits in 56 consecutive games. ✳ The New York Yankees defeat the Brooklyn Dodgers to take the World Series. **MISCELLANEOUS**: Mount Rushmore National Monument completed.

1942

FAMILY
Milestones

CATALOG *of Sources*

HEADLINE: U.S. defeats Japan in Battles of the Coral Sea and Midway. **MILITARY**: Establishment of the WAAC, SPARS, WAFS and WAVES. ✷ U.S. troops invade North Africa. ✷ U.S. Marines use Navajo Code Talkers in the Pacific theatre. ✷ Tokyo and other Japanese cities are bombed by Major Doolittle's planes. ✷ U.S. troops die in the Bataan Death March. ✷ The first Liberty ships are put into service. ✷ S.N.A.F.U., one of many military acronyms. **CIVIL RIGHTS**: Executive order 9066 interns 110,000 Japanese-Americans. ✷ CORE, the Congress of Racial Equality, is founded. **RELIGION**: Father Divine moves his "heaven" from Harlem to Philadelphia. **SCIENCE**: The first controlled nuclear chain reaction is achieved at the University of Chicago. **INVENTIONS**: Magnetic recording tape introduced. **NEW PRODUCTS**: Hoarding due to rationing of food stuffs and essentials. ✷ Victory Gardens are cultivated. **TRANSPORTATION**: The last automobile until the end of WWII rolls off the assembly line. **BOOKS**: *Go Down Moses* by William Faulkner; *The Little House* by Virginia Lee Burton. **THEATER**: *This is the Army*, a musical by Irving Berlin. **MUSIC**: *White Christmas*; *That Old Black Magic*; *Don't Sit Under the Apple Tree*; *Jingle Jangle Jingle*. ✷ *Chattanooga Choo-Choo* becomes the first "gold record." **RADIO**: *People are Funny*; *Suspense*. **FILM**: *Mrs. Miniver*, starring Greer Garson and Walter Pidgeon; *Casablanca* with Humphrey Bogart and Ingrid Bergman; *Yankee Doodle Dandy* with James Cagney. **FASHIONS**: The introduction of polyesters for clothing. ✷ Sales of women's trousers skyrocket. **SPORTS**: The St. Louis Cardinals defeat the New York Yankees in the World Series. **MISCELLANEOUS**: Introduction of Daylight Savings Time.

1943

FAMILY
Milestones

CATALOG *of Sources*

CATALOG *of Sources*

HEADLINE: U.S. living standard is one-third higher than in 1939. **GOVERNMENT**: Congress passes a "Pay-As-You Go" Tax Payment Act. **MILITARY**: Among Allied victories are the invasions of Sicily and Italy in Europe, and the Battle of the Bismarck Sea and Guadalcanal in the Pacific. ✳ Roosevelt, Churchill and Stalin meet in Teheran to plan war strategy. ✳ Liberty ships are completed in 4 days. ✳ Cartoonist Bill Mauldin draws "Willie and Joe" for the Army newspaper *Stars and Stripes*. ✳ The Pentagon is completed. **HEALTH**: The antibiotic streptomycin is discovered by Selman Waksman. ✳ The Pap test for detecting cervical cancer is recognized by the medical establishment. **INVENTIONS**: Continuous casting is introduced to steel manufacturing. **NEW PRODUCTS**: Americans must "use it up, wear it out, make it do or do without." **COMMUNICATION**: ABC is founded by Edward Noble. **BOOKS**: *A Tree Grows in Brooklyn* by Betty Smith; *The Fountainhead* by Ayn Rand. **THEATER**: *Oklahoma* and *Carmen Jones* are new musicals. **ART**: *The Hunter*, painting by Andrew Wyeth. ✳ Edward Chavez completes the mural *Indians of the Plains*. **MUSIC**: *Mairzy Doats*; *Hey, Good Lookin*; *I'll Be Home for Christmas*; *Oh, What a Beautiful Morning*. **DANCES**: The jitterbug is the popular dance. **RADIO**: *Perry Mason* and *Nick Carter, Master Detective*. **FILM**: *The Ox-Bow Incident* with Henry Fonda and Dana Andrews; *Heaven Can Wait* with Gene Tierney and Don Ameche. **SPORTS**: Count Fleet takes the Triple Crown. ✳ Protective helmets are now required in professional football. ✳ The New York Yankees defeat the St. Louis Cardinals to take the World Series.

1944

CATALOG *of Sources*

FAMILY *Milestones*

HEADLINE: The Supreme Court rules that Americans cannot be denied the vote due to color. **GOVERNMENT**: FDR elected to 4th term, Harry Truman elected VP. **MILITARY**: Battles in Europe include D-Day at Normandy, Anzio Beach in Italy and the Battle of the Bulge. In the Pacific, U.S. forces bomb Japan, win in the Battle of the Philippine Sea and MacArthur returns to the Philippines. **EDUCATION**: Congress passes the GI Bill of Rights. **HEALTH**: DDT is used to control body lice. **RELIGION**: Evangelist Aimee Semple McPherson dies from a drug overdose. **SCIENCE**: A digital computer is built at Harvard University. ✳ DNA is isolated by Oswald Avery. **NEW PRODUCTS**: Kodak introduces Kodacolor film. **ECONOMICS**: The World Bank and The International Monetary Fund are created. **BOOKS**: *Strange Fruit* by Lillian Smith. **MAGAZINES**: *Seventeen* magazine begins publication. **THEATER**: The ballet *Appalachian Spring* by Aaron Copland with choreography by Martha Graham; Tennessee Williams' play *The Glass Menagerie*. **MUSIC**: *Sentimental Journey*; *Would You Like to Swing on a Star?*; *Don't Fence Me In*; *This Land Is Your Land*. **RADIO**: *The Adventures of Ozzie and Harriet*; *Roy Rogers*. **FILM**: *National Velvet* with Mickey Rooney and Elizabeth Taylor; *Arsenic and Old Lace* with Priscilla Lane and Josephine Hull; *Going My Way* with Bing Crosby. **FASHIONS**: Both men's and women's clothing features broad padded shoulders. ✳ Besides bobbysocks, teens wear baggy jeans with shirttails hanging out. **SPORTS**: The St. Louis Cardinals defeat the St. Louis Browns to take the World Series.

1945

CATALOG *of Sources*

FAMILY *Milestones*

HEADLINE: World War II ends when Germany surrenders on May 8 and Japan surrenders on September 2. **GOVERNMENT**: Roosevelt dies; Harry Truman is sworn in as President. **MILITARY**: The first atomic bomb, "Little Boy," is dropped on Hiroshima Aug. 6 by the *Enola Gay*. ✳ Total WWII deaths are about 55,000,000. ✳ Korea is divided between U.S. and Soviet occupation forces along the 38th parallel. **TRAGEDY**: A B-25 bomber crashes into the Empire State Building. **HEALTH**: Streptomycin and penicillin become commercially available. ✳ The introduction of water fluoridation to prevent cavities. **ORGANIZATIONS**: CARE (Co-operative for American Relief Everywhere) is founded. **SCIENCE**: German rocket engineer Wernher von Braun continues his research in the U.S. ✳ White Sands, NM, is the site of the first atomic detonation. **NEW PRODUCTS**: Aerosol spray cans, ballpoint pens and Tupperware are introduced. ✳ The manufacture of consumer goods resumes and food rationing ends. **COMMUNICATION**: The FCC sets aside channels for commercial TV. **BOOKS**: *Up Front* by Bill Mauldin; *Cannery Row* by John Steinbeck; *Stuart Little* by E.B. White; *Forever Amber* by Kathleen Winsor. **MAGAZINES**: *Ebony* magazine begins publication. **THEATER**: *Carousel*, a musical by Rodgers and Hammerstein. **MUSIC**: *It's a Grand Night for Singing*; *Let It Snow!*; *He's Got the Whole World in His Hands*. **RADIO**: *Queen For a Day, Meet the Press*. **FILM**: *The Lost Weekend* with Ray Milland and Jane Wyman; *Spellbound* by Alfred Hitchcock. **SPORTS**: The Detroit Tigers defeat the Chicago Cubs to take the World Series. ✳ The American Football League is organized. **FADS**: Introduction of the Slinky toy.

1946

CATALOG *of Sources*

FAMILY *Milestones*

HISTORICAL *Context of 1946*

HEADLINE: Truman seizes mines and railroads as millions of workers strike for better pay. **GOVERNMENT**: The Atomic Energy Commission is established. **MILITARY**: The beginning of the "cold war." ✷ War criminals are tried at Nuremberg, Germany. **CIVIL RIGHTS**: Congress establishes the Indian Claims Commission. **EDUCATION**: Fulbright scholarships are established. **RELIGION**: Mother Frances X. Cabrini is the first U.S. citizen to be canonized a saint. **ECOLOGY**: A-bomb tests at Bikini Atoll. **INVENTIONS**: ENIAC, the first digital computer goes on line. ✷ Printed circuits are developed. **NEW PRODUCTS**: *Timex* watches and *Tide* are introduced. **ECONOMICS**: Consumers demonstrate against inflation when price and wage controls are lifted. **BUSINESS**: "Bugsy" Siegel builds the Flamingo Hotel in Las Vegas, NV. **BOOKS**: *I, the Jury* by "Mickey" Spillane; *The Egg and I* by Betty MacDonald; *The Common Sense Book of Baby and Child Care* by Dr. Benjamin Spock. **THEATER**: *The Iceman Cometh* by Eugene O'Neill. *Annie Get Your Gun* with Ethel Merman. **ART**: *Out for Christmas Trees*, painted by Grandma Moses. **MUSIC**: *Route 66*; *Zip-a-Dee-Do-Dah*; *Doin' What Comes Natur'lly*. ✷ Fender Guitar Co. invents the solid body electric guitar. **RADIO**: *Sam Spade* is a popular new program. ✷ The first full time Spanish language station KCOR-AM is established in San Antonio, TX. **FILM**: *It's a Wonderful Life* with James Stewart and Donna Reed. **FASHIONS**: The bikini is introduced. **SPORTS**: The automatic pinspotter is introduced to bowling. ✷ The St. Louis Cardinals defeat the Boston Red Sox to take the World Series. ✷ Golfer Betty Berg wins the first Women's U.S. Open. **POPULATION**: Birthrates begin to soar.

1947

CATALOG *of Sources*

FAMILY *Milestones*

HEADLINE: The "Hollywood Ten" are imprisoned for refusing to affirm or deny their membership in the Communist Party. **GOVERNMENT**: The Truman Doctrine of Soviet containment is introduced. ✳ NSC and CIA established. **CIVIL RIGHTS**: Mexican-American veterans organize the American GI Forum. **LABOR**: The Taft-Hartley Act, which forbids closed shops, is passed. ✳ A "cost-of-living" raise is agreed upon by GM and the UAW. **ORGANIZATIONS**: The Ford Foundation is established. **RELIGION**: Billy Graham begins preaching at revival meetings. **SCIENCE**: The Bell X-1 rocket plane breaks the sound barrier. ✳ Radiocarbon dating is developed. **NEW PRODUCTS**: The introduction of Ajax, the Toni permanent and the Polaroid Land Camera. **FOOD**: Reddi Wip and Almond Joy are introduced. **TRANSPORTATION**: The first tubeless tires appear. **COMMUNICATION**: The first microwave relay station begins operation. **ECONOMICS**: Average salary is $2,600. The average teacher salary is $2,250. **BOOKS**: *Gentleman's Agreement* by Laura Z. Hobson; *McElliot's Pool* by Dr. Seuss. **THEATER**: *A Streetcar Named Desire* by Tennessee Williams. **ART**: *Full Fathom Five*, a drip painting by Jackson Pollock. **MUSIC**: *I'm Looking Over a Four-Leaf Clover*; *Papa, Won't You Dance With Me?* **FILM**: *Miracle on 34th Street* with Natalie Wood and Maureen O'Hara; *The Ghost and Mrs. Muir* with Gene Tierney and Rex Harrison. **TV**: *Kraft Television Theatre, Howdy Doody, Meet the Press*. **FASHIONS**: American women buy into Christian Dior's lowered skirt lengths, padded bras, unpadded shoulders and fezzes. **SPORTS**: The New York Yankees defeat the Brooklyn Dodgers in the first TV broadcast of the World Series. ✳ The Brooklyn Dodgers sign up Jackie Robinson. **FADS**: The first report of "flying saucers" begins a craze.

1948

CATALOG *of Sources*

FAMILY *Milestones*

HEADLINE: U.S. begins the Berlin Airlift after the Soviets seal off the city. **GOVERNMENT**: Harry Truman and Alben Barkley are elected president and VP. **MILITARY**: The Selective Service Act becomes law. **CIVIL RIGHTS**: Truman desegregates the Armed Forces. **EDUCATION**: The Supreme court declares religious education in public schools unconstitutional. **ORGANIZATIONS**: International Planned Parenthood Federation is founded. **SCIENCE**: Mathematician Norbert Wiener introduces "cybernetics." ✳ The telescope at Mount Palomar is dedicated. **INVENTIONS**: The transistor is invented by a Bell Lab research team. **NEW PRODUCTS**: Dramamine and Dial deodorant soap are introduced. **TRANSPORTATION**: Air-conditioning is offered for automobiles. **ECONOMICS**: U.S. becomes a net importer of oil. ✳ Congress authorizes the Marshall Plan to help rebuild Europe. **BUSINESS**: The first McDonald's restaurant opens. **BOOKS**: *The Naked and the Dead* by Norman Mailer. **MAGAZINES**: *U.S. News and World Report* begins publication. **THEATER**: The New York City Ballet presents *Orpheus* with Maria Tallchief and Nicholas Magallanes. **ART**: *Christina's World*, a painting by Andrew Wyeth. **MUSIC**: *If I Had a Hammer*; *Nature Boy*; *Tennessee Waltz*; *Smoke, Smoke, Smoke That Cigarette*. ✳ LP records are introduced. **RADIO**: *Stop the Music*; *This Is Your Life*. **FILM**: *The Treasure of the Sierra Madre* by John Huston. **TV**: *Kukla, Fran & Ollie*; *The Milton Berle Show*; *Hopalong Cassidy*; *The Ed Sullivan Show*; *The Perry Como Show*. **SPORTS**: The Cleveland Indians defeat the Boston Red Sox to take the World Series. ✳ Golfer Ben Hogan wins the U.S. Open. **FADS**: The Pez candy dispenser and the game Scrabble are introduced. **NOTORIETY**: Whittaker Chambers accuses Alger Hiss of being a communist. **MISCELLANEOUS**: The comic strip "Pogo" debuts.

1949

FAMILY
Milestones

CATALOG *of Sources*

HISTORICAL *Context of 1949*

HEADLINE: General Motors, Standard Oil of California, Firestone Tire and other companies are convicted of criminal conspiracy to replace electric transit lines with gasoline or diesel buses. **MILITARY**: NATO is established. **CIVIL RIGHTS**: Edith Mae Irby is the first Negro admitted to the University of Arkansas Medical School. **LABOR**: Minimum wage set at $.75 per hour. **EXPLORATION**: *Lucky Lady II* completes first circumglobal nonstop flight. **COMMUNICATION**: Radio Free Europe begins broadcasting. **BOOKS**: *The Hero With a Thousand Faces* by Joseph Campbell; *Cheaper by the Dozen* by Frank Gilbreth, Jr., and Ernestine Gilbreth. **THEATER**: *Death of a Salesman* by Arthur Miller; *South Pacific*, a musical by Rodgers and Hammerstein. **MUSIC**: Miles Davis cuts the first "cool" jazz records. ✶ *Rudolph, the Red-Nosed Reindeer*; *Ghost Riders in the Sky*; *Diamonds Are a Girl's Best Friend*; *Mona Lisa*. **RADIO**: New programs include *Dragnet*. **FILM**: *Adam's Rib* with Spencer Tracy and Katharine Hepburn; *Twelve O'Clock High* with Gregory Peck; *On the Town* with Gene Kelly and Frank Sinatra. **TV**: *The Goldbergs*; *The Life of Riley*; *Red Barber's Corner*; *Crusader Rabbit*; *Captain Video and His Video Rangers*; *The Lone Ranger*. ✶ Gorgeous George becomes one of the first TV sports celebrities. **SPORTS**: The New York Yankees defeat the Brooklyn Dodgers to take the World Series. ✶ Golfer Sam Snead wins the Masters Tournament. ✶ The National Basketball Association (NBA) is formed. **FADS**: Silly Putty is introduced. **NOTORIETY**: Tokyo Rose goes on trial.

1950

FAMILY
Milestones

HEADLINE: The Korean War begins when North Korea invades South Korea. **MILITARY**: Truman authorizes the development of a hydrogen bomb. **CRIME**: A Brink's robbery in Boston nets over $1.2 million. **LABOR**: Truman orders the Army to seize the railroads. **ORGANIZATIONS**: Congress establishes the National Science Foundation. **NEW PRODUCTS**: DuPont introduces Orlon. ✻ Xerox copying machines and Otis self-service elevators are introduced. **FOOD**: *Minute Rice* and *Sugar Pops* are introduced. **BOOKS**: *I, Robot* by Isaac Asimov; *Betty Crocker's Picture Cook Book*. **THEATER**: The play *Guys and Dolls* opens. **MUSIC**: *Good Night, Irene*; *I Wanna Be Loved*; *Rag Mop*; *Silver Bells*. **DANCES**: The mambo is introduced from Cuba. **FILM**: *All About Eve* with Bette Davis; *Sunset Boulevard* with Gloria Swanson. **TV**: Sen. Estes Kefauver of Tennessee becomes famous by holding hearings into organized crime on TV. ✻ Color television broadcasting begins. ✻ *The Gene Autry Show*; *What's My Line?*; *The Jack Benny Show*; *Truth or Consequences*; *The Steve Allen Show*; *The George Burns and Gracie Allen Show*. **FASHIONS**: The D.A. hair style is popular with young men. **SPORTS**: The New York Yankees defeat the Philadelphia Phillies to take the World Series. ✻ The Minneapolis Lakers defeat the Syracuse Nationals for the NBA Championship. **FADS**: *Dianetics: The Modern Science of Mental Healing* by L. Ronald Hubbard. **NOTORIETY**: Sen. Joe McCarthy begins a 4-year episode of character assassination. **FAME**: Smokey the Bear is rescued after a fire in New Mexico. **MISCELLANEOUS**: Charles Schulz creates "Peanuts." **POPULATION**: The U.S. population is 150,697,361. ✻ 1,035,039 immigrants entered the U.S. in the last decade.

1951

CATALOG *of Sources*

FAMILY *Milestones*

HISTORICAL *Context of 1951*

HEADLINE: Truman relieves MacArthur of his military duties. **GOVERNMENT**: The adoption of 22nd Amendment which limits a president to two terms. **MILITARY**: 250,000 GIs are in Korea. ✴ The U.S. begins testing nuclear devices with live troops. **TRAGEDY**: Flooding in Kansas and Missouri leaves 200,000 homeless. **ECOLOGY**: *The Sea Around Us*, a book by Rachel Carson, begins the environmental movement. **SCIENCE**: The first power-producing nuclear reactor goes on line. **INVENTIONS**: UNIVAC, with a 1.5K memory, is the first commercial computer. **BUSINESS**: Texas Instruments Incorporates. **BOOKS**: *The Catcher in the Rye* by J.D. Salinger; *From Here to Eternity* by James Jones. **THEATER**: *The King and I*, a musical by Rodgers and Hammerstein. **MUSIC**: The *Dave Brubeck Quartet* is formed. ✴ *On Top of Old Smoky*; *Mockin' Bird Hill*; *Getting to Know You*; *Kisses Sweeter Than Wine*; *Unforgettable*. **FILM**: *The African Queen* with Humphrey Bogart and Katharine Hepburn; *A Streetcar Named Desire* with Marlon Brando and Vivian Leigh; *The Day the Earth Stood Still* with Michael Rennie and Patricia Neal. **TV**: *The Cisco Kid*; *I Love Lucy*; *Superman*; *Search for Tomorrow*; *Watch Mr. Wizard*; *The Roy Rogers Show*; *The Red Skelton Show*. ✴ The first transcontinental TV broadcast is an address by Truman. **FASHIONS**: Teenage girls wear poodle skirts and saddle shoes. **SPORTS**: Sugar Ray Robinson wins the middleweight title. ✴ The New York Yankees defeat the New York Giants to take the World Series. ✴ Golfer Ben Hogan wins the Masters Tournament. **MISCELLANEOUS**: Americans begin building personal bomb shelters. ✴ Hank Ketcham introduces "Dennis the Menace."

1952

CATALOG *of Sources*

FAMILY *Milestones*

HEADLINE: Dwight D. Eisenhower and Richard M. Nixon are elected president and VP. **MILITARY**: The H-bomb is exploded at Eniwetok. ✱ Eisenhower visits Korea. **EDUCATION**: "Subversives" are prohibited from teaching in public schools. **HEALTH**: A polio epidemic afflicts 50,000 Americans. ✱ Jonas Salk develops a polio vaccine. **ORGANIZATIONS**: John D. Rockefeller, Jr., founds the Population Council. **RELIGION**: Lucille Ball's pregnancy on her TV show is approved by a minister, a priest and a rabbi. ✱ *Revised Standard Version of the Bible* is published. **SCIENCE**: The "Big Bang" theory is described. **NEW PRODUCTS**: Sony introduces pocket-sized transistor radios. ✱ The first videotape is demonstrated. ✱ The Palmer Paint Company introduces paint-by-number kits. **TRANSPORTATION**: The number of diesel-electric trains surpasses steam locomotives. **BUSINESS**: The first Holiday Inn opens in Memphis, TN. **BOOKS**: *The Old Man and the Sea* by Ernest Hemingway; *Player Piano* by Kurt Vonnegut; *Charlotte's Web* by E.B. White. **MAGAZINES**: *Mad* magazine begins publication. **MUSIC**: *You Belong to Me*; *Tell Me Why*; *Your Cheatin' Heart*; *Jambalaya—in the Bayou*. **FILM**: *High Noon* with Gary Cooper and Grace Kelly; *Singin' in the Rain* with Gene Kelly. **TV**: *The Adventures of Ozzie & Harriet*; *Death Valley Days*; *Dragnet*; *The Today Show*; *American Bandstand*; *I've Got a Secret*. ✱ 70 million watch the Republican and Democratic conventions. **SPORTS**: The New York Yankees defeat the Brooklyn Dodgers to take the World Series. ✱ U.S. athletes clean up at the Helsinki Winter Olympics. **FADS**: Kids wear beanies with propellers. ✱ Panty-raids become popular on college campuses. **NOTORIETY**: Richard Nixon makes his "Checkers" speech.

1953

CATALOG *of Sources*

FAMILY
Milestones

HEADLINE: A Korean armistice is signed; U.S. casualties include 25,604 dead. **GOVERNMENT**: Earl Warren becomes Chief Justice of the Supreme Court. **HEALTH**: Transistorized hearing aids are introduced. ✶ Alfred Kinsey publishes his study: *Sexual Behavior in the Human Female*. ✶ The heart-lung machine is developed. **RELIGION**: The Marilyke tagging system is introduced for Catholic girls to dress modestly. ✶ L. Ron Hubbard founds the Church of Scientology. **ECOLOGY**: Nuclear fallout from an atomic test rains down on St. George, UT. **SCIENCE**: Watson and Crick decode the DNA double helix. **INVENTIONS**: Physicist Charles Townes develops the MASER. **FOOD**: TV dinners, instant iced tea and Sugar Smacks are introduced. **BUSINESS**: Lawrence Ferlinghetti opens City Lights Bookshop in San Francisco. **BOOKS**: *Go Tell It on the Mountain* by James A. Baldwin; *The Power of Positive Thinking* by Norman Vincent Peale. **MAGAZINES**: *Playboy* and *TV Guide* debut. **THEATER**: *The Crucible* by Arthur Miller debuts. **MUSIC**: *That's Amore*; *Doggie in the Window*; *Vaya Con Dios*. **FILM**: *Gentlemen Prefer Blondes* with Jane Russell and Marilyn Monroe; *Shane* with Alan Ladd and Jean Arthur; *From Here to Eternity* with Deborah Kerr and Burt Lancaster. **TV**: *Flash Gordon*; *General Electric Theatre*; *The Loretta Young Show*; *Romper Room*. ✶ KUHI is the first educational TV station. **FASHIONS**: Bermuda shorts are promoted for men, toreador pants for women. **SPORTS**: The New York Yankees defeat the Brooklyn Dodgers for the World Series. ✶ Golfer Ben Hogan wins the U.S. Open and Masters tournaments. **NOTORIETY**: Charlie Chaplin is banned from the U.S. **MISCELLANEOUS**: Meteorologists give women's names to hurricanes.

1954

FAMILY
Milestones

HEADLINE: The Supreme Court outlaws segregation in public schools in *Brown v. Board of Education of Topeka, KS*. **GOVERNMENT**: Five Congressmen are shot by Puerto Rican nationalists. **MILITARY**: *U.S.S. Nautilus* is the first atomic submarine. ✳ U.S. and Canada announce construction of the DEW (Distant Early Warning) radar network. **EDUCATION**: Mississippians vote to abolish public schools to halt integration. **HEALTH**: The first successful kidney transplant. ✳ Children are inoculated with Salk's polio vaccine. **RELIGION**: Eisenhower changes the *Pledge of Allegiance* to include the words "under God." **ECOLOGY**: H-bomb fallout from Bikini Atoll rains on Micronesia. **INVENTIONS**: Photovoltaic cells and silicon transistors are introduced. **TRANSPORTATION**: Introduction of the Ford Thunderbird and the Chevrolet Corvette. ✳ Construction of the St. Lawrence Seaway begins. **BUSINESS**: Ray Kroc buys franchise rights from McDonald's. **BOOKS**: *The Blackboard Jungle*, a novel by Evan Hunter. ✳ *The Life of John Birch* by Robert H.W. Welch. **MAGAZINES**: *Sports Illustrated* begins publication. ✳ Comic-book publishers adopt Comics Code. **MUSIC**: *Sh-Boom*; *Mister Sandman*; *Shake, Rattle and Roll*; *That's All Right, Mama*. **DANCES**: The cha-cha is popularized. **FILM**: *The Wild One* with Marlon Brando; *The Bridges at Toko-Ri* with William Holden. **TV**: RCA markets color TVs. ✳ *Father Knows Best*; *The Tonight Show*; *Lassie*; *The Jimmy Durante Show*; *People Are Funny*; *Walt Disney Show*. **SPORTS**: Golfer Ed Furgol wins the men's U.S. Open. ✳ The New York Giants defeat the Cleveland Indians to take the World Series. **FADS**: Fess Parker starts the Davy Crockett craze. **OCCASIONS**: The Iwo Jima Memorial Monument is dedicated in Washington, D.C. **NOTORIETY**: Edward R. Murrow denounces Sen. Joe McCarthy.

1955

FAMILY *Milestones*

HISTORICAL *Context of 1955*

HEADLINE: Albert Sabin develops an oral polio vaccine. Polio cases drop sharply as a result of vaccination. **MILITARY**: U.S. begins sending aid to Southeast Asia. ✴ U.S. Air Force Academy opens. **CIVIL RIGHTS**: Rosa Parks refuses to give up her bus seat in Montgomery, AL. **LABOR**: The AFL and CIO merge. **HEALTH**: Gregory Pincus discovers an oral contraceptive. **RELIGION**: The Presbyterian Church approves ordination of women ministers. ✴ Rock-n-roll music is declared "immoral" by moralists. **INVENTIONS**: Velcro, optical fibers and synthetic diamonds are introduced. **NEW PRODUCTS**: Crest toothpaste and Special K are introduced. **TRANSPORTATION**: Container ships begin to revolutionize the cargo-shipping industry. **BUSINESS**: Disneyland opens in Anaheim, CA. ✴ H & R Block and Kentucky Fried Chicken are founded. **BOOKS**: *Auntie Mame* by Patrick Dennis; *Frog Went a-Courtin'* by John Langstaff; *Howl* by Allen Ginsberg. **THEATER**: *Cat on a Hot Tin Roof* by Tennessee Williams. **MUSIC**: *Rock Around the Clock*; *Sixteen Tons*; *Maybellene*; *Memphis*; *Love and Marriage*; *Roll Over, Beethoven*. **FILM**: *Rebel Without a Cause* with James Dean and Natalie Wood; *Blackboard Jungle* with Glenn Ford and Ann Francis. ✴ James Dean is killed in car wreck. **TV**: Mary Martin stars in the TV spectacular *Peter Pan*. ✴ *The Lawrence Welk Show*; *Captain Kangaroo*; *Sheena, Queen of the Jungle*; *Soupy Sales*; *Gunsmoke*; *The Honeymooners*; *The Phil Silvers Show*. ✴ Jim Henson creates Kermit the Frog. **FASHIONS**: Pink suddenly appears in menswear. **SPORTS**: The Brooklyn Dodgers defeat the New York Yankees to take the World Series. **FADS**: Automobile stuffing becomes popular on college campuses.

1956

FAMILY
Milestones

CATALOG *of Sources*

HEADLINE: Dwight D. Eisenhower and Richard Nixon are re-elected president and VP. **MILITARY**: The last Union Army veteran from the Civil War, Albert Woolson, dies at 109. ✳ The Polaris missile is developed. **TRAGEDY**: The *Andrea Doria* sinks off Nantucket Island. **HEALTH**: "Hiroshima Maidens" receive plastic surgery treatment for radiation burns. **ORGANIZATIONS**: The La Leche League International, Inc., is founded. **RELIGION**: Methodist Church abolishes racism in its churches. **SCIENCE**: The subatomic neutrino is observed. **NEW PRODUCTS**: Robert Adler invents the TV remote control. ✳ Stainless-steel razor blades, Pampers and Comet cleanser are introduced. **TRANSPORTATION**: The Interstate Highway program is authorized. **COMMUNICATION**: The first transatlantic telephone cable becomes operational. **BUSINESS**: Midas Muffler opens. ✳ Ringling Brothers & Barnum and Bailey Circus folds. **BOOKS**: *Profiles in Courage* by John F. Kennedy. **THEATER**: *My Fair Lady* with Julie Andrews and Rex Harrison. **MUSIC**: *Heartbreak Hotel*; *Blue Suede Shoes*; *Love Me Tender*; *Blueberry Hill*; *Que Será, Será*; *Hound Dog*. ✳ *Mass* by Leonard Bernstein. **FILM**: *The King and I* with Yul Brynner and Deborah Kerr; *The Ten Commandments* with Charlton Heston and Yul Brynner. **TV**: 54 million watch Elvis on the *Ed Sullivan Show*. ✳ *Broken Arrow*; *The Dinah Shore Chevy Show*; *As the World Turns*; *To Tell the Truth*; *Dick Powell's Zane Grey Theatre*. **FASHIONS**: Crew cuts and flat tops are popular. ✳ Short shorts become acceptable. **SPORTS**: Floyd Patterson takes the heavyweight title. ✳ The New York Yankees defeat the Brooklyn Dodgers to take the World Series. **FAME**: Actress Grace Kelly marries Prince Rainier III of Monaco.

1957

CATALOG *of Sources*

FAMILY
Milestones

HEADLINE: Federal troops desegregate Central High School in Little Rock, AR. **MILITARY**: An ICBM (intercontinental ballistic missile) is successfully tested. **CRIME**: New York's "Mad Bomber" is arrested. **CIVIL RIGHTS**: A civil rights bill passes Congress. **LABOR**: Jimmy Hoffa becomes head of the Teamsters Union. **ORGANIZATIONS**: American scientists urge a ban on nuclear weapon tests. **SCIENCE**: Scientists from 67 nations participate in the International Geophysical Year. **NEW PRODUCTS**: Spandex and stereo recordings are introduced. **TRANSPORTATION**: Ford Motor Co. introduces the Edsel. **ECONOMICS**: President Eisenhower extends the Truman Doctrine to cover the Mideast. **BOOKS**: *On the Road* by Jack Kerouac; *Atlas Shrugged* by Ayn Rand; *The Cat in the Hat* by Dr. Seuss. **THEATER**: *West Side Story* by Sondheim, Bernstein and Robbins. **MUSIC**: *Jailhouse Rock*; *Wake Up Little Susie*; *Peggy Sue*; *A White Sport Coat and a Pink Carnation*; *Whole Lotta Shakin' Goin' On'*. **FILM**: *Bridge on the River Kwai* with William Holden; *And God Created Woman* with Brigitte Bardot; *The Incredible Shrinking Man* by Jack Arnold. **TV**: *Leave It to Beaver*; *Perry Mason*; *Wagon Train*; *The Twentieth Century*; *Have Gun Will Travel*; *The Real McCoys*; *The Gumby Show*; *American Bandstand*. **FASHIONS**: Black leather jackets are popular with teenage boys. ✳ Plaid sport jackets are introduced for men. ✳ The sack dress is introduced. **SPORTS**: The Milwaukee Braves defeat the New York Yankees to take the World Series. ✳ The Boston Celtics defeat the St. Louis Hawks for the NBA Championship. **FADS**: Wham-O introduces the Hula Hoop and Frisbee. **MISCELLANEOUS**: The first large nuclear power plant goes on line.

1958

FAMILY
Milestones

CATALOG *of Sources*

HEADLINE: *Nautilus* makes the first undersea crossing of North Pole. **MILITARY**: U.S. Troops are sent to Lebanon. ✳ The first U.S. ICBM is successfully launched. **TRAGEDY**: 87 children die in a fire at Our Lady of the Angels School in Chicago. **CRIME**: Charles Starkweather and his girlfriend are arrested after a killing spree. **EDUCATION**: The U.S. National Defense Education Act is passed to promote science and math. **HEALTH**: Ultrasound is first used to examine an unborn fetus. **ORGANIZATIONS**: Robert Welch founds the John Birch Society. ✳ NASA is established. **SCIENCE**: U.S. launches its first satellite. ✳ The Van Allen radiation belts are discovered. **INVENTIONS**: The integrated circuit is invented. **FOOD**: Sweet'n Low sweetener is introduced. **TRANSPORTATION**: The FAA is established to ensure air safety. ✳ The Boeing 707 goes into service. **COMMUNICATION**: United Press International is created. **ECONOMICS**: Americard (now Visa) and the American Express card are introduced. **BUSINESS**: The first Pizza Hut opens in Kansas City. **BOOKS**: *Breakfast at Tiffany's* by Truman Capote. **MUSIC**: *At the Hop*; *Tom Dooley*; *Yakety Yak*; *Purple People Eater*; *Catch a Falling Star*; *Fever*. ✳ Van Cliburn wins the Tchaikovsky piano competition in Moscow. **FILM**: *Vertigo* by Alfred Hitchcock. **TV**: *Naked City*; *The Rifleman*; *Huckleberry Hound*; *The Donna Reed Show*; *Maverick*; *77 Sunset Strip*. ✳ *The Nine Lives of Elfago Baca* by Walt Disney. **FASHIONS**: The "beatnik" look calls for dark clothes. **SPORTS**: The New York Yankees defeat the Milwaukee Braves to take the World Series. ✳ Golfer Arnold Palmer wins the Masters tournament. **NOTORIETY**: The Liz-Eddie-Debbie Love Triangle is a Hollywood scandal.

1959

CATALOG *of Sources*

FAMILY *Milestones*

HISTORICAL *Context of 1959*

HEADLINE: Nixon and Soviet Premier Khrushchev engage in a "kitchen debate" in Moscow. **GOVERNMENT**: Alaska and Hawaii enter Union as 49th and 50th states. **MILITARY**: The first U.S. military advisors die in Vietnam. ✱ Walter Williams, the last Confederate soldier dies at age 117. **EXPLORATION**: NASA selects the first seven U.S. astronauts. **INVENTIONS**: The microchip is invented. **FOOD**: Tang is marketed. **TRANSPORTATION**: American Motors introduces Rambler to compete with the small foreign cars. ✱ The St. Lawrence Seaway is opened. **BOOKS**: *Exodus* by Leon Uris; *Hawaii* by James A. Michener. **THEATER**: *Raisin in the Sun* by Lorraine Hansberry **ART**: Robert Rauschenberg creates *Monogram*, a "combine" painting. **MUSIC**: *Stagger Lee*; *The Battle of New Orleans*; *High Hopes*; *Mack The Knife*; *Venus*. ✱ Buddy Holly, Ritchie Valens and the Big Bopper die in a plane crash. ✱ Berry Gordy founds Motown Records. **FILM**: *Ben Hur* with Charlton Heston; *Some Like It Hot* with Marilyn Monroe, Tony Curtis and Jack Lemmon. **TV**: *Rawhide*; *The Twilight Zone*; *The Untouchables*; *Bonanza*; *The Many Loves of Dobie Gillis*; *Rocky and His Friends*. **FASHIONS**: Pantyhose are introduced by Glen Raven Mills. **SPORTS**: The Los Angeles Dodgers defeat the Chicago White Sox to take the World Series. ✱ Ingemar Johansson KOs Floyd Patterson for the heavyweight title. ✱ The Boston Celtics defeat the Minneapolis Lakers for the NBA Championship. **FADS**: The Barbie doll is introduced. ✱ Telephone-booth-stuffing is the rage on college campuses. **NOTORIETY**: The "great quiz show scandal" involves individuals who were coached before the shows.

1960

CATALOG *of Sources*

FAMILY *Milestones*

HEADLINE: John F. Kennedy and Lyndon Johnson are elected president and VP. **GOVERNMENT**: Eisenhower warns against the "military-industrial-complex," while Kennedy campaigns to close the "missile gap." **MILITARY**: The Soviets shoot down a U-2 spy plane. ✳ *U.S.S. Triton* completes the first undersea circumnavigation of the globe. **CIVIL RIGHTS**: African-Americans sit-in at lunch counters to force desegregation. **HEALTH**: An oral contraceptive, "the Pill," is marketed. **RELIGION**: Maharishi Mahesh Yogi begins teaching TM (transcendental meditation) in the U.S. ✳ Pat Robertson founds the Christian Broadcasting Network. **SCIENCE**: *Tiros I* and *Echo I* are launched. ✳ Quasars are discovered. **INVENTIONS**: Demonstration of a laser. **FOOD**: Soft drinks are marketed in aluminum cans. **TRANSPORTATION**: The U.S. has over 2.17 million miles of surfaced road. **BOOKS**: *To Kill a Mockingbird* by Harper Lee; *Island of the Blue Dolphin* by Scott O'Dell. **MUSIC**: *Itsy Bitsy Teenie Weenie Yellow Polka Dot Bikini*; *Are You Lonesome To-Night?*; *A Summer Place*; *Georgia on My Mind*; *Teen Angel*. **DANCES**: Chubby Checker introduces the twist. **FILM**: *Psycho* with Anthony Perkins and Janet Leigh; *Spartacus* by Stanley Kubrick with Kirk Douglas. **TV**: Nixon and Kennedy debate on TV. ✳ Popular new shows are *The Andy Griffith Show*; *The Flintstones*; *My Three Sons*. **FASHIONS**: Jackie Kennedy becomes a model of good taste in fashion. ✳ Pierced ears become acceptable. **SPORTS**: The Pittsburgh Pirates defeat the New York Yankees to take the World Series. ✳ U.S. Olympic hockey team brings home the gold. **MISCELLANEOUS**: The Playboy Bunny debuts. **POPULATION**: The U.S. population is 179,245,000. ✳ 2,515,479 immigrants entered the U.S. in the previous decade.

1961

FAMILY
Milestones

HISTORICAL *Context of 1961*

HEADLINE: Alan Shepard is the first American in space. * Kennedy challenges the Soviets to a Race to the Moon **MILITARY**: After the failed "Bay of Pigs" invasion, Washington severs relations with Cuba. * Kennedy begins to increase the U.S. military presence in Vietnam. **CRIME**: Hijacking of planes to Cuba. **CIVIL RIGHTS**: CORE Freedom Riders are beaten as they test segregation in the south. **HEALTH**: The FDA approves acetaminophen. * Smoking is linked to heart disease. * The drug thalidomide is found to cause birth defects. **ORGANIZATIONS**: President Kennedy creates the Peace Corps. **RELIGION**: The National Council of Churches endorses birth control. **ECOLOGY**: 17 million acres of virgin wilderness remain in the U.S. **INVENTIONS**: IBM introduces the Selectric typewriter. **NEW PRODUCTS**: The electric toothbrush is introduced. **BOOKS**: *Catch-22* by Joseph Heller; *Stranger in a Strange Land* by Robert Heinlein. **ART**: Roy Lichtenstein paints, *Look, Mickey*. **MUSIC**: *Calcutta*; *Travelin' Man*; *Where Have All the Flowers Gone*; *Moon River*. * Bob Dylan begins his recording career. **FILM**: *Breakfast at Tiffany's* with Audrey Hepburn; *The Parent Trap* with Hayley Mills. **TV**: *Ben Casey*; *The Dick Van Dyke Show*; *Wide World of Sports, Dr. Kildare*; *Mr. Ed* * The FCC Chairman. calls TV "a vast wasteland." * SIN (Spanish International Network) is established. **FASHIONS**: "Greasy kid stuff" is out of style. * The beehive hairdo is popular. **SPORTS**: Roger Maris hits 61 home runs. * The New York Yankees defeat the Cincinnati Reds to take the World Series. **FADS**: Every boy needs a yo-yo.

1962

FAMILY
Milestones

CATALOG *of Sources*

HISTORICAL *Context of 1962*

HEADLINE: The Cuban Missile Crisis brings the U.S. and the Soviet Union to the brink of war. **MILITARY**: U.S. advisors in Vietnam are allowed to return fire. **TRAGEDY**: Marilyn Monroe dies from a drug overdose. **CIVIL RIGHTS**: James Meredith is the first African-American student to enroll at the University of Mississippi. **LABOR**: Cesar Chavez leads the National Farm Workers Association in California. **HEALTH**: Eye surgery is performed using a laser. **ECOLOGY**: Rachel Carson publishes *Silent Spring*. **EXPLORATION**: John Glenn is the first American to orbit the earth. **FOOD**: *Diet-Rite* is the first diet soda marketed. **COMMUNICATION**: *Telstar I* transmits live telecasts between the U.S. and Britain. **BUSINESS**: The first Kmart and Wal-Mart stores open. **BOOKS**: *A Wrinkle in Time* by Madeleine L'Engle; *One Flew Over the Cuckoo's Nest* by Ken Kesey. **ART**: *The Twenty Marilyns* by Andy Warhol. **MUSIC**: *I Can't Stop Loving You*; *Big Girls Don't Cry*; *Duke of Earl*; *Johnny Angel*; *Blowin' in the Wind*. ✳ *The First Family* an album by Vaughn Meader. **FILM**: *Dr. No* with Sean Connery and Ursula Andress; *What Ever Happened to Baby Jane?* with Bette Davis and Joan Crawford. **TV**: *The Merv Griffin Show*; *Beverly Hillbillies*; *McHale's Navy*; *Beany and Cecil*; *The Tonight Show* starring Johnny Carson. **FASHIONS**: Teenage boys wear pointy shoes with cuban heels. **SPORTS**: Wilt Chamberlain scores 100 points in a single basketball game. ✳ Sonny Liston defeats Floyd Patterson for the heavyweight title. ✳ The New York Yankees defeat the San Francisco Giants to take the World Series.

1963

FAMILY
Milestones

HEADLINE: John F. Kennedy is assassinated in Dallas, TX; Lyndon Johnson becomes President. **GOVERNMENT**: The U.S. and the USSR set up a "hot line" to prevent accidental nuclear war. **TRAGEDY**: The *U.S.S. Thresher* sinks with all men aboard. **CIVIL RIGHTS**: 200,000 march on Washington to demonstrate for civil rights. ✳ NAACP leader Medgar Evers is murdered. ✳ The Supreme Court rules that accused criminals have the right to free counsel. **EDUCATION**: New Hampshire institutes a state lottery to raise money for education. **HEALTH**: The first lung and liver transplants are performed. **RELIGION**: The Catholic Church approves vernacular languages for the Mass. **ECOLOGY**: U.S. Clean Air Act becomes law. **INVENTIONS**: Digital introduces a successful minicomputer. **NEW PRODUCTS**: *Instamatic* cameras, aluminum pop-top cans, *Touch-Tone* phones and skateboards are introduced. **BOOKS**: *The Feminine Mystique* by Betty Friedan; *Where the Wild Things Are* by Maurice Sendak. **ART**: *Whaam!* cartoon art by Roy Lichtenstein. **MUSIC**: *Dominique*; *Sugar Shack*; *Surfin' U.S.A.*; *He's So Fine*; *My Boyfriend's Back*; *If I Had a Hammer*; *Puff (the Magic Dragon)*. **FILM**: *Cleopatra* with Elizabeth Taylor, Rex Harrison and Richard Burton; *The Nutty Professor* with Jerry Lewis. **TV**: *The Fugitive*; *My Favorite Martian*; *Tennessee Tuxedo and His Tales*; *Petticoat Junction*. **SPORTS**: The Los Angeles Dodgers defeat the New York Yankees to take the World Series. ✳ The Boston Celtics defeat the Los Angeles Lakers for the NBA Championship. ✳ Arnold Palmer is the first professional golfer to earn over $100,000 a year. **FADS**: Hootenannies become popular. ✳ *Ratfink* by Ed "Bigdaddy" Roth.

1964

CATALOG *of Sources*

FAMILY *Milestones*

HISTORICAL *Context of 1964*

HEADLINE: Lyndon Johnson and Hubert Humphrey are elected president and VP. **GOVERNMENT**: The food stamp program begins. ✳ The Warren Commission report on the JFK assassination is released. **MILITARY**: Congress approves the Tonkin Gulf Resolution, thereby escalating the Vietnam war. **CIVIL RIGHTS**: Southern senators filibuster for 75 days before the Civil Rights Act is passed. ✳ Dr. Martin Luther King, Jr. receives the Nobel Peace Prize. **HEALTH**: The Surgeon General links cigarette smoking with cancer. **ORGANIZATIONS**: Head Start is established. **ECOLOGY**: Congress passes the Wilderness Act. **NEW PRODUCTS**: Hasbro introduces G.I. Joe. **TRANSPORTATION**: Ford introduces the Mustang. **ECONOMICS**: President Johnson calls for a war on poverty. **BOOKS**: *The Spy Who Came in From the Cold* by John Le Carré; *Games People Play* by Eric Berne. **THEATER**: *Hello, Dolly!* with Carol Channing; *Funny Girl* with Barbra Streisand. **MUSIC**: *I Want to Hold Your Hand*; *Baby Love*; *I Get Around*; *Oh, Pretty Woman*; *Love Potion No. 9*; *Name Game*; *Stop in the Name of Love*; *She Loves You*. **DANCES**: Monkey, chicken, watusi and frug. **FILM**: *Dr. Strangelove* by Stanley Kubrick; *Mary Poppins* with Julie Andrews and Dick Van Dyke. **TV**: *Bewitched*; *Gilligan's Island*; *Underdog*; *The Addams Family*; *The Man From U.N.C.L.E.* **FASHIONS**: Beatlemania makes long hair fashionable for men. **SPORTS**: The St. Louis Cardinals defeat the New York Yankees to take the World Series. ✳ Cassius Clay defeats Sonny Liston for the heavyweight title. **FADS**: Troll dolls peak in popularity. **MISCELLANEOUS**: The St. Louis Arch is completed.

1965

FAMILY *Milestones*

CATALOG *of Sources*

HISTORICAL *Context of 1965*

HEADLINE: Operation Rolling Thunder escalates the Vietnam War as B-52s selectively bomb North Vietnam. **GOVERNMENT**: Johnson outlines his "Great Society" program. **MILITARY**: Antiwar protests break out, draft cards are burned. **CIVIL RIGHTS**: State police attack civil rights demonstrators in Selma, AL. ✳ Congress passes the Voting Rights Act. ✳ Malcom X assassinated. **EDUCATION**: College students and faculty discuss Vietnam at "teach-ins." **HEALTH**: Medicare is established. ✳ "Caution: Cigarette smoking may be hazardous to your health." is required on cigarette packs. **ORGANIZATIONS**: National Endowment for the Humanities is created. **RELIGION**: Swami Prabhupada founds the International Society for Krishna Consciousness. **EXPLORATION**: The first U.S. spacewalk. **SCIENCE**: The cosmic background radiation predicted by the "Big Bang" Theory is verified. **ECONOMICS**: The new "clad" coins conserve silver. ✳ Mexico and the U.S. initiate the Maquiladora Program. **BOOKS**: *Unsafe at Any Speed* by Ralph Nader; *Dune* by Frank Herbert; *The Psychedelic Reader* by Timothy Leary. **ART**: Op art goes mainstream. **MUSIC**: *Help!*; *Mr. Tambourine Man*; *Wooly Bully*; *I Got You Babe*; *King of the Road*; *(I Can't Get No) Satisfaction*; *Yesterday*; *Help Me, Rhonda*. ✳ *The Grateful Dead* forms. **FILM**: *The Pawnbroker* with Rod Steiger; *The Sound of Music* with Julie Andrews and Christopher Plummer. **TV**: *Get Smart*; *Green Acres*; *I Dream of Jeannie*; *Hogan's Heroes*; *Lost in Space*. **FASHIONS**: Mary Quant introduces the miniskirt. ✳ The "afro" becomes popular with young African-Americans. **SPORTS**: The Los Angeles Dodgers defeat the Minnesota Twins to take the World Series. **FADS**: Body painting and macrobiotic foods have followers. **MISCELLANEOUS**: Power blackout in Northeast. ✳ "Flower Power."

1966

CATALOG *of Sources*

FAMILY *Milestones*

HISTORICAL *Context of 1966*

HEADLINE: The Supreme Court issues the Miranda Ruling. **MILITARY**: Four H-Bombs fall from a B-52 over Spain. ✳ The Vietnam War continues. **CRIME**: Richard Speck murders 8 student nurses in Chicago. ✳ Charles Whitman shoots 12 people at the University of Texas at Austin. **ORGANIZATIONS**: The Black Panther Party is organized. ✳ The National Organization for Women is founded. **RELIGION**: Catholics are now allowed to eat meat on Fridays. **ECOLOGY**: The first endangered species list is produced. **EXPLORATION**: *Surveyor I* lands on moon. **FOOD**: New food items include Taster's Choice instant coffee and Bac-Os. **TRANSPORTATION**: The Motor Vehicle Safety Act is passed. **BOOKS**: *Sam, Bangs & Moonshine* by Evaline Ness; *In Cold Blood* by Truman Capote; *The Valley of the Dolls* by Jacqueline Susann; *Human Sexual Response* by Masters and Johnson. **MUSIC**: *Yellow Submarine*; *Monday, Monday*; *The Sounds of Silence*; *Devil With the Blue Dress*; *Mellow Yellow*. ✳ *Freak Out*, an album by Frank Zappa. **DANCES**: "Acid rock" dance halls have light shows accompanying acid rock music. **FILM**: *Fantastic Voyage* with Raquel Welch; *Who's Afraid of Virginia Woolf?* with Richard Burton and Elizabeth Taylor. **TV**: *Family Affair*; *Batman*; *Star Trek*. **SPORTS**: The Baltimore Orioles defeat the Los Angeles Dodgers to take the World Series. ✳ Golfer Al Beiberger wins the PGA. **FADS**: The German Iron Cross becomes a short-term fad with the beach set. **MISCELLANEOUS**: The architecturally innovative Atlanta Hyatt Regency Hotel, with a 22-story atrium, opens. ✳ Stokely Carmichael promotes the Black Power movement.

1967

FAMILY Milestones

CATALOG of Sources

HEADLINE: Thurgood Marshall becomes first African-American on the Supreme Court. **MILITARY**: 474,000 U.S. troops are in Vietnam. ✷ 700,000 march in an antiwar protest in New York City. **TRAGEDY**: Three astronauts are killed in the *Apollo I* fire. **CIVIL RIGHTS**: The CIA illegally begins "Operation Chaos" to spy on antiwar activities and the "Stop the Draft" movement. **EDUCATION**: Tennessee's "Monkey Law" is repealed. **HEALTH**: The first coronary bypass operation is performed. **ORGANIZATIONS**: The Corporation for Public Broadcasting is created. **SCIENCE**: Biologically active DNA is synthesized. **INVENTIONS**: The atomic second becomes the time standard. **NEW PRODUCTS**: Amana introduces a household microwave oven. **BOOKS**: *Christy* by Catherine Marshall. **MAGAZINES**: *Rolling Stone* begins publication. **MUSIC**: *Ode to Billie Joe*; *The Letter*; *Light My Fire*; *Somebody to Love*. ✷ Albums include *Sgt. Pepper's Lonely Hearts Club Band* by the Beatles; *Alice's Restaurant* by Arlo Guthrie. ✷ Monterey, CA is the site of the first rock festival. **FILM**: *The Graduate* by Mike Nichols; *Bonnie and Clyde* with Warren Beatty and Faye Dunaway. **TV**: *The Smothers Brothers Comedy Hour*; *Ironside*. **FASHIONS**: Granny glasses, nehru jackets and antiwar buttons make the scene. **SPORTS**: Arnold Schwarzenegger wins the Mr. Universe title. ✷ The Green Bay Packers defeat Kansas City Chiefs in the first Super Bowl. ✷ The St. Louis Cardinals defeat the Boston Red Sox to take the World Series. **FADS**: Psychedelic posters and "Head Shops" appear. **FAME**: Dr. Martin Luther King, Jr. encourages draft evasion. ✷ Dr. Spock is arrested for antiwar activities ✷ Muhammad Ali refuses induction into the armed forces.

1968

FAMILY Milestones

CATALOG of Sources

HEADLINE: Robert F. Kennedy and Dr. Martin Luther King, Jr. are assassinated. **GOVERNMENT**: Richard Nixon and Spiro Agnew are elected president and VP. ✳ Chicago police beat demonstrators at the Democratic National Convention. **MILITARY**: U.S. troops massacre civilians at My Lai. ✳ The Vietcong launches the Tet Offensive. **CIVIL RIGHTS**: Riots occur in over 125 cities following King's assassination. **EDUCATION**: Yale admits women. **ORGANIZATIONS**: AIM, the American Indian Movement, is founded. ✳ La Raza Unida is organized. **ECOLOGY**: 6,000 sheep next to Dugway Proving Ground die from nerve gas exposure. **SCIENCE**: Pulsars are discovered. ✳ Enzymes which cut DNA strands at certain points are discovered. **NEW PRODUCTS**: The Jacuzzi Whirlpool is introduced. **BUSINESS**: Automated teller machines are introduced. **BOOKS**: *The Whole Earth Catalog* by Stewart Brand; *The Electric Kool-Aid Acid Test* by Tom Wolfe; *In Watermelon Sugar* by Richard Brautigan. **THEATER**: *Hair*, a rock musical. **MUSIC**: Some songs include: *Hey Jude*; *(Sittin' On) The Dock of the Bay*; *Mrs. Robinson*; *Love Child*; *Harper Valley PTA*. ✳ The Beatles' "White Album" is released. **FILM**: *Yellow Submarine* by George Duning; *2001: A Space Odyssey* by Stanley Kubrick; *Bullitt* with Steve McQueen. ✳ The G, M, R and X movie-rating system is introduced. **TV**: *Hawaii Five-O*; *Rowan & Martin's Laugh-In*; *Julia*; *60 Minutes*. **FASHIONS**: The "Mod" and "Hippie" looks are in. **SPORTS**: The Detroit Tigers defeat the St. Louis Cardinals to take the World Series. ✳ Arthur Ashe wins the U.S. Open in Tennis. **MISCELLANEOUS**: Robert Crumb publishes *Zap Comix*. ✳ Congress recommends that the U.S. adopt the Metric system.

1969

FAMILY Milestones

CATALOG of Sources

HEADLINE: Neil Armstrong and Buzz Aldrin land on the moon. **GOVERNMENT**: The trial of the "Chicago 8" begins. ✳ Black Panthers Fred Hampton and Mark Clark are killed during a Chicago police raid. **MILITARY**: Millions of Americans protest the Vietnam war during Vietnam Moratorium Day. ✳ B-52s secretly bomb Communist bases in Cambodia. **CRIME**: Sharon Tate and companions are murdered by the Manson cult. **CIVIL RIGHTS**: New York's Stonewall Inn riot launches a "gay rights" movement. **HEALTH**: MSG is banned from baby food. ✳ Mother's breast milk is found to contain four times the allowable level of DDT. **ORGANIZATIONS**: The Weather Underground (Weathermen) breaks from the SDS. **INVENTIONS**: The first microprocessor is invented. **BOOKS**: *Sounder* by William Armstrong; *Portnoy's Complaint* by Philip Roth; *Slaughterhouse-Five* by Kurt Vonnegut. **MAGAZINES**: *Penthouse* magazine begins publication. **THEATER**: *Oh! Calcutta!* by Kenneth Tynan. **MUSIC**: *Honky Tonk Women*; *Spinning Wheel*; *Sugar, Sugar*; *Good Morning Starshine*; *Okie from Muskogee*. ✳ 400,000 attend Woodstock Music and Art Fair. **FILM**: *Easy Rider* by Dennis Hopper; *True Grit* with John Wayne. **TV**: *The Brady Bunch*; *Hee Haw*; *Love American Style*; *Sesame Street*. ✳ *The Smothers Brothers Comedy Hour* and *Star Trek* canceled. ✳ Tiny Tim and Miss Vicki marry on the *Tonight Show*. **FASHIONS**: Tie-dyeing, pant suits for women and bell-bottom pants become fashionable. **SPORTS**: The New York Jets defeat the Baltimore Colts to take the Super Bowl. **NOTORIETY**: Mary Jo Kopechne dies when the car driven by Edward Kennedy crashes off the Chappaquiddick Bridge. **MISCELLANEOUS**: The cartoon strip "Doonesbury" debuts.

1970

FAMILY
Milestones

CATALOG of Sources

HISTORICAL *Context of 1970*

HEADLINE: Four student protestors are killed by National Guardsmen at Kent State University. **GOVERNMENT**: Wage and price freezes are instituted. ✳ Passage of the Water Quality and Clean Air Acts. **MILITARY**: The Vietnam peace talks in Paris continue. **TRAGEDY**: Hard hats break up an antiwar rally in the Wall Street area. **CIVIL RIGHTS**: President Nixon restores the sacred Blue Lake to Taos Pueblo. **HEALTH**: Linus Pauling endorses Vitamin C to treat colds. **ECOLOGY**: 20 million Americans observe April 21 as Earth Day. **EXPLORATION**: *Apollo 13* returns safely to earth. **SCIENCE**: The first synthetic gene is created. ✳ The first black hole is located. **INVENTIONS**: Floppy disks are introduced to store computer data. **NEW PRODUCTS**: Safety caps appear on drug and other product containers. **TRANSPORTATION**: The Boeing 747 begins commercial service. **BOOKS**: *Sexual Politics* by Kate Millett; *Future Shock* by Alvin Toffler; *The Greening of America* by Charles Reich. **MUSIC**: *Bridge Over Troubled Water*; *We've Only Just Begun*; *Let It Be*. ✳ Albums include: *Abraxas* by Santana; *Blows Against the Empire* by Paul Kantner. **FILM**: *Love Story* with Ryan O'Neal and Ali MacGraw; *M*A*S*H* by Robert Altman. **TV**: *Monday Night Football*; *The Mary Tyler Moore Show*; *The Partridge Family*; *Evening at Pops*; *All My Children*. **FASHIONS**: Girdles and bras lose favor with younger women. **SPORTS**: The Baltimore Orioles defeat the Cincinnati Reds to take the World Series. ✳ The first New York City Marathon attracts 126 starters. **POPULATION**: The U.S. population is 203,302,031. ✳ 3,321,677 immigrants entered the U.S. in the previous decade.

1971

CATALOG *of Sources*

FAMILY
Milestones

CATALOG *of Sources*

HISTORICAL *Context of 1971*

HEADLINE: The Supreme Court upholds busing of schoolchildren to achieve racial balance. **GOVERNMENT**: 18 becomes the voting age. **MILITARY**: The Vietnam War drags on. **CRIME**: Several thousand Vietnam veterans throw away their medals on the Capitol steps to protest the War. ✱ The *New York Times* publishes the "Pentagon Papers." **LABOR**: The Brotherhood of Locomotive Engineers lets railroads scrap the 100 miles a day rule. **ORGANIZATIONS**: The first Rainbow Family gathering. **INVENTIONS**: Intel introduces a microprocessor. **NEW PRODUCTS**: Texas Instruments introduces the pocket calculator. **TRANSPORTATION**: Amtrak takes over most U.S. passenger rail traffic. **ECONOMICS**: Nixon imposes freeze on rents, wages and prices, and devalues dollar. **BOOKS**: *Mrs. Frisby and the Rats of NIMH* by Robert C. O'Brien; *Bury My Heart at Wounded Knee* by Dee Brown; *The Drifters* by James Michener. **THEATER**: *Jesus Christ Superstar* by Andrew Lloyd Webber. **MUSIC**: *Bad Moon Rising*; *Green River*. ✱ *Imagine* an album by John Lennon. **RADIO**: *All Things Considered* debuts. **FILM**: *Summer of '42* with Jennifer O'Neill; *Shaft* by Gordon Parks; *Dirty Harry* with Clint Eastwood. **TV**: *All in the Family*; *Columbo*; *The Sonny and Cher Comedy Hour*; *Masterpiece Theater*. ✱ Cigarette advertisements are banned from TV. **FASHIONS**: Hot Pants appear for one season. ✱ Young men and women custom patch their jeans. **SPORTS**: Joe Frazier beats Muhammad Ali for the heavyweight title. ✱ The Pittsburgh Pirates defeat the Baltimore Orioles to take the World Series. ✱ The Baltimore Colts defeat the Dallas Cowboys to win the Super Bowl.

1972

CATALOG *of Sources*

FAMILY *Milestones*

HEADLINE: Richard M. Nixon and Spiro Agnew are re-elected president and VP. **GOVERNMENT**: Nixon goes to China to establish political ties. ✹ The National Commission on Marijuana and Drug Abuse urges an end to criminal penalties for private use and possession of marijuana. **MILITARY**: B-52s bomb Hanoi and Haiphong. ✹ The military draft ends, and the armed services become all-volunteer. **CRIME**: Five burglars are arrested at Democratic Party Headquarters in the Watergate Hotel. **HEALTH**: Hexachlorophene is banned. **RELIGION**: Sally J. Priesand becomes the first woman rabbi in U.S. **ECOLOGY**: Congress passes a Water Pollution Control Act. **ECONOMICS**: Nearly one-third of the petroleum consumed is imported. ✹ The Soviets buy one-fourth of the U.S. wheat crop. **BUSINESS**: Federal Express and Nike, Inc., are founded. **BOOKS**: *Julie of the Wolves* by Jean C. George; *The Foxfire Book* by Eliot Wigginston; *Bless Me, Ultima* by Rudolfo Anaya. **MAGAZINES**: Gloria Steinem founds *Ms.* magazine. **ART**: *Indians to Rockets*, a mural by Luis Jimenez. **MUSIC**: *Alone Again (Naturally)*; *American Pie*; *A Horse With No Name*; *I Am Woman*. **FILM**: *The Godfather* by Francis Ford Coppola; *Cabaret* by Bob Fosse; *The Poseidon Adventure* by Irwin Allen. **TV**: *M*A*S*H*; *Kung Fu*; *Sanford and Son*; *Maude*; *Fat Albert and the Cosby Kids*; *The Waltons*. **SPORTS**: Mark Spitz wins seven gold medals at the Munich Olympics. ✹ The Dallas Cowboys defeat the Miami Dolphins to win the Super Bowl. **FADS**: Acupuncture is popularized. **FAME**: Woodward and Bernstein of the *Washington Post* crack the Watergate affair. ✹ Bobby Fischer beats Russian chess champion Boris Spassky.

1973

FAMILY
Milestones

CATALOG *of Sources*

HEADLINE: The Supreme Court decision in *Roe v. Wade* legalizes abortion. **GOVERNMENT**: VP Spiro Agnew resigns amid charges of income tax evasion. ✳ Gerald Ford is sworn in as VP. **MILITARY**: Direct U.S. ground troop involvement in Vietnam ends. **CRIME**: Senator Sam Ervin, Jr. heads the committee to investigate Watergate. **ACTIVISIM**: Members of the American Indian Movement occupy Wounded Knee, SD. **LABOR**: Farm labor represents 5 percent of U.S. work force. **HEALTH**: A CAT scan machine is introduced. ✳ Homosexuality is no longer classified as a mental disorder. ✳ Marijuana is used to treat glaucoma. **SCIENCE**: The Skylab is launched. **NEW PRODUCTS**: The Cuisinart kitchen machine is introduced to the U.S. ✳ The Universal Product Code label is recommended by the grocery industry. **ECONOMICS**: The first Arab oil embargo. ✳ The U.S. dollar is devalued 10 percent. **BOOKS**: *The Slave Dancer* by Paula Fox; *Gravity's Rainbow* by Thomas Pynchon; *Fear of Flying* by Erica Jong; *Breakfast of Champions* by Kurt Vonnegut. **MUSIC**: *You're So Vain*; *We're an American Band*; *Killing Me Softly With His Song*; *Rocky Mountain High*; *Delta Dawn*. **FILM**: *The Exorcist* with Linda Blair; *American Graffiti* by George Lucas. **TV**: *Barnaby Jones*; *The Six Million Dollar Man*; *The Midnight Special*. **FASHIONS**: Silk screened T-shirts are accepted as casual wear. ✳ Southwestern Indian jewelry becomes a fashion statement. **SPORTS**: Billie Jean King beats Bobby Riggs in a "Battle of the Sexes." ✳ Miami Dolphins defeat the Washington Redskins to win the Super Bowl. **MISCELLANEOUS**: Chicago's Sears Tower becomes the world's tallest building at 1,455 feet (440m).

1974

CATALOG *of Sources*

FAMILY *Milestones*

HEADLINE: The House Judiciary Committee votes to impeach President Nixon. ✳ President Nixon resigns; Gerald Ford becomes the 38th president. **GOVERNMENT**: President Gerald Ford grants Richard Nixon a pardon. ✳ Congress passes an election reform act and a Freedom of Information Act. **TRAGEDY**: Karen Silkwood dies in an auto crash on the road to a meeting with a reporter to expose nuclear power cover-ups. **CRIME**: The Symbionese Liberation Army kidnaps Patricia Hearst. **HEALTH**: The Heimlich Maneuver is popularized. **RELIGION**: Some cult followers are rescued and deprogrammed. **SCIENCE**: The National Academy of Sciences urges a ban on some genetic manipulation. **TRANSPORTATION**: A 55 mph highway speed limit law goes into effect. ✳ Motorists experience gasoline shortages. **COMMUNICATION**: Word processors come into use. **ECONOMICS**: The ban on ownership of gold is lifted. ✳ Money markets become available to small investors. **BOOKS**: *Arrow to the Sun* by Gerald McDermott; *Carrie* by Stephen King; *Jaws* by Peter Benchley. **MUSIC**: *The Streak*; *Band on the Run*; *Sunshine on My Shoulder*; *I Shot the Sheriff*. **FILM**: *Young Frankenstein* by Mel Brooks; *Chinatown* with Jack Nicholson and Faye Dunaway. **TV**: *Rhoda*; *The Rockford Files*; *Happy Days*; *Chico and the Man*; *Police Woman*. **FASHIONS**: The string bikini debuts. **SPORTS**: Jimmy Connors wins the U.S. Open in tennis. ✳ Hank Aaron breaks Babe Ruth's career homerun record. ✳ The Miami Dolphins defeat the Minnesota Vikings to win the Super Bowl. **FADS**: "Streaking" has a brief exposure on college campuses. **MAGAZINES**: *High Times* magazine and *People* magazine begin publication.

1975

CATALOG *of Sources*

FAMILY *Milestones*

HEADLINE: Mayhem breaks out as the U.S. evacuates Saigon. The Vietnam War ends. **GOVERNMENT**: President Ford escapes two assassination attempts. ✳ President Ford signs the Metric Conversion Act. ✳ Revelations that secret files were kept on American citizens by the CIA and FBI. **MILITARY**: Deaths in the Vietnam War: 1.3 million. **LABOR**: Jimmy Hoffa disappears. **HEALTH**: Lyme disease is identified in Lyme, CT. **RELIGION**: Chief Frank Fools, a Native American holy man, offers prayers to open the U.S. Senate. **ECOLOGY**: The Toxic Substances Control Act phases out PCBs. **EXPLORATION**: *Apollo 18* docks with *Soyuz 19*. **NEW PRODUCTS**: Digital watches and VCRs are introduced. **FOOD**: Lite beers are marketed. **ECONOMICS**: Unemployment is 9 percent. **BUSINESS**: Bill Gates and Paul Gardner Allen found Microsoft. **BOOKS**: *The Monkey Wrench Gang* by Edward Abbey; *Shogun* by James Clavell. **THEATER**: *A Chorus Line*, a musical by Michael Bennett. **MUSIC**: *Have You Never Been Mellow*; *Fame*; *My Eyes Adored You*. ✳ *Born to Run*, an album by Bruce Springsteen. **DANCES**: The Hustle and Bump are popular in discos. **FILM**: *The Man Who Would Be King* by John Huston; *Jaws* with Roy Scheider. **TV**: *MacNeil/Lehrer News Hour*; *The Jeffersons*; *NBC's Saturday Night Live*; *Mary Hartman, Mary Hartman*. **FASHIONS**: Jumpsuits appear as casual wear. ✳ "Designer" jeans and gold neckchains become popular. **SPORTS**: O.J. Simpson scores 23 touchdowns this season. ✳ Muhammad Ali beats Joe Frazier in the "Thrilla in Manila." ✳ Chris Evert wins the women's U.S. Open in Tennis. **FADS**: CB radios gain popularity. ✳ The "Pet Rock" sells for the season. **MISCELLANEOUS**: Vietnamese "boat people" arrive in the U.S.

1976

FAMILY
Milestones

CATALOG *of Sources*

HISTORICAL *Context of 1976*

HEADLINE: Jimmy Carter and Walter Mondale are elected president and VP. **GOVERNMENT**: The Supreme Court rules that capital punishment does not constitute "cruel and unusual punishment." ✳ California enacts a "right-to-die" law. **MILITARY**: Cruise missiles are developed. **EDUCATION**: Rhodes Scholarships become available to women **RELIGION**: The Rev. Sun Myung Moon ends his ministry in the U.S. **EXPLORATION**: The *Viking I* spacecraft lands on Mars. **FOOD**: High fiber foods become popular. ✳ Red Dye No. 2 is banned. ✳ The first cases of Legionnaires' disease occur in Philadelphia. **TRANSPORTATION**: Automobile mileage standards are mandated. **COMMUNICATION**: FAX machines become common. **BUSINESS**: Genentech, Apple Computer and WTBS in Atlanta are founded. ✳ Drexel Burnham Lambert is founded to deal in "junk bonds." **BOOKS**: *Interview With the Vampire* by Anne Rice; *Roots* by Alex Haley. **ART**: *Running Fence* by Christo is a cloth wall 24 miles long. **MUSIC**: *Tonight's the Night*; *Silly Love Songs*; *Don't Go Breaking My Heart*; *I Write the Songs*; *50 Ways to Leave Your Lover*. **FILM**: *Rocky* with Sylvester Stallone; *Taxi Driver* with Robert DeNiro; *The Bad News Bears* by Michael Ritchie. **TV**: *Charlie's Angels*; *Laverne & Shirley*; *The Bionic Woman*; *The Muppet Show*. **FASHIONS**: Dorothy Hamill haircuts are popular. **SPORTS**: The Cincinnati Reds defeat the New York Yankees to take the World Series. ✳ The Pittsburgh Steelers defeat the Dallas Cowboys to win the Super Bowl. **FADS**: Farrah Fawcett-Majors posters are big sellers. ✳ EST is the latest form of self-realization. **MISCELLANEOUS**: Bicentennial celebrations take place across the nation.

1977

CATALOG *of Sources*

FAMILY *Milestones*

HISTORICAL *Context of 1977*

HEADLINE: Fluorocarbons are banned as aerosol propellants. **GOVERNMENT**: President Carter pardons Vietnam War draft evaders. ✳ Carter makes "human rights" a part of U.S. foreign policy. ✳ Tokyo Rose is pardoned. **MILITARY**: The neutron bomb is developed. **CRIME**: Gary Gilmore is the first person to be executed in the U.S. since 1967. **CIVIL RIGHTS**: Leonard Peltier of AIM is convicted of killing two FBI agents and sentenced to prison. **HEALTH**: Balloon angioplasty is developed for opening clogged arteries. ✳ Insulin is produced from genetically engineered bacteria. **SCIENCE**: The MRI (Magnetic Resonance Imaging) scanner is developed. **NEW PRODUCTS**: The *Apple II* personal computer is marketed. ✳ VHS recorders are introduced. **COMMUNICATION**: Lawyers are now allowed to advertise. **BOOKS**: *Bridge to Terabithia* by Katherine Paterson; *The Thorn Birds* by Colleen McCullough. **MUSIC**: *You Light Up My Life*; *Best of My Love*; *A Star Is Born*; *You Make Me Feel Like Dancing*. ✳ *Hotel California* an album by the Eagles is released. ✳ Elvis, "The King," Presley, dies. **FILM**: *Close Encounters of the Third Kind* by Steven Spielberg; *Star Wars* by George Lucas; *The Turning Point* by Herbert Ross. **TV**: *The Love Boat*; *Soap*; *Chips*; *Three's Company*. ✳ *Roots*, a miniseries, breaks records for audience size. **SPORTS**: Jockey Steve Cauthen rides a record 487 winners. ✳ Janet Guthrie is the first woman to race in the Indianapolis 500. ✳ The Portland Trailblazers defeat the Philadelphia 76ers for the NBA Championship. **FADS**: Billy Beer flops as a fad. ✳ Hacky Sack is introduced. **MISCELLANEOUS**: *Gossamer Condor* is the first human-powered plane.

1978

FAMILY
Milestones

CATALOG *of Sources*

HEADLINE: Californians revolt against high taxes and approve Proposition 13. **GOVERNMENT**: The U.S. and Panama renew the Panama Canal treaties. **TRAGEDY**: Jim Jones orders his cult followers to commit mass suicide at the People's Temple, Jonestown, Guyana. **HEALTH**: Interferon is prematurely hailed as a cure for some cancers. **RELIGION**: The American Indian Religious Freedom Act is passed. **EXPLORATION**: The *Double Eagle II* is the first balloon to cross the Atlantic. **TRANSPORTATION**: The Airline Deregulation Act begins a phase-out of regulations. **ECONOMICS**: Money market funds are popular hedge against the high inflation rate. **BUSINESS**: Gambling casinos open in Atlantic City, NJ. **MUSIC**: *Mammas Don't Let Your Babies Grow Up to Be Cowboys*; *Shadow Dancing*; *Le Freak*; *Three Times a Lady*. **FILM**: *The Deer Hunter* by Michael Cimino; *Superman* with Christopher Reeve; *Halloween* with Jamie Lee Curtis; *National Lampoon's Animal House* with John Belushi. **TV**: *Dallas*; *Fantasy Island*; *The Incredible Hulk*; *Mork & Mindy*; *20/20*; *WKRP in Cincinnati*. **FASHIONS**: Jogging outfits for fashionable workouts. **SPORTS**: Mario Andretti wins the Formula One Grand Prix. ✳ The Dallas Cowboys defeat the Denver Broncos to win the Super Bowl. ✳ The New York Yankees defeat the Los Angeles Dodgers to take the World Series. **FADS**: Due to the TV miniseries *Roots*, genealogy becomes popular. **MISCELLANEOUS**: Jim Davis introduces the cartoon strip "Garfield."

1979

FAMILY
Milestones

CATALOG *of Sources*

HEADLINE: 52 hostages are taken when the U.S. embassy in Iran is seized. **GOVERNMENT**: The Camp David Peace Accord between Israel and Egypt is engineered by President Carter. ✳ Washington establishes diplomatic relations with Beijing. **TRAGEDY**: A near meltdown occurs at Three Mile Island nuclear plant. **CIVIL RIGHTS**: U.S. Supreme Court upholds affirmative action. **EDUCATION**: The Department of Education attains Cabinet level status. **HEALTH**: The first case of AIDS is diagnosed. **ORGANIZATIONS**: Jerry Falwell founds the *Moral Majority*, a political action group. **SCIENCE**: A black hole is discovered at the center of our galaxy. **NEW PRODUCTS**: Reebok shoes are introduced. **TRANSPORTATION**: Gasoline rationing goes into effect as the oil embargo takes hold. **ECONOMICS**: The inflation rate is 13.3 percent. ✳ A $1.5 billion federal loan guarantee plan is approved for Chrysler Corporation. **BUSINESS**: Lisa Frank, Inc., is founded. **BOOKS**: *Sophie's Choice* by William Styron; *The Gnostic Gospels* by Elaine Hiesey Pagels; *The Right Stuff* by Tom Wolfe. **MUSIC**: *Rapper's Delight*; *Bad Girls*; *Too Much Heaven*; *Heartache Tonight*; *My Sharona*. **RADIO**: *A Prairie Home Companion* and *Morning Edition* debut on NPR. **FILM**: *Apocalypse Now* by Francis Ford Coppola; *Alien* with Sigourney Weaver; *Cheech and Chong's Up in Smoke* with Cheech and Chong. **TV**: *Little House on the Prairie*; *Knots Landing*; *Dukes of Hazzard*. **SPORTS**: The Pittsburgh Pirates defeat the Baltimore Orioles to take the World Series. ✳ Tracy Austin wins the women's U.S. Open in tennis. **FADS**: Sony introduces the *Walkman*. **MISCELLANEOUS**: *Skylab* crashes to earth.

1980

FAMILY
Milestones

CATALOG *of Sources*

HISTORICAL *Context of 1980*

HEADLINE: Ronald Reagan and George Bush are elected president and VP. **MILITARY**: A military mission to rescue the U.S. hostages in Iran fails. **CRIME**: ABSCAM uncovers bribery of public officials. **HEALTH**: Pregnant women are encouraged to avoid caffeine. ✱ Toxic Shock Syndrome is reported. **ECOLOGY**: The EPA superfund is created. ✱ Love Canal, NY, is declared a disaster area due to toxic waste. **EXPLORATION**: Max and Kris Anderson cross North America on a nonstop balloon flight. **SCIENCE**: The Supreme Court rules that genetically engineered life may be patented. **NEW PRODUCTS**: Cordless telephones become widely available. **COMMUNICATION**: AT&T begins marketing 900 numbers. **ECONOMICS**: The banking industry is deregulated. ✱ The Hunt brothers of Dallas fail to corner the silver market. **BUSINESS**: Honda announces plans to build an auto plant in the U.S. **BOOKS**: *Cosmos* by Carl Sagan; *Firestarter* by Stephen King; *Clan of the Cave Bear* by Jean M. Auel. **MUSIC**: *Lady*; *Magic*; *Funkytown*. ✱ John Williams becomes conductor of the Boston Pops Orchestra. ✱ Former Beatle, John Lennon, is shot to death. **FILM**: *The Empire Strikes Back* by Irvin Kershner; *Airplane* by Jim Abrahams. **TV**: CNN (Cable Network News) begins broadcasting. ✱ New shows include *Magnum P.I.*; *Nightline*; *Too Close for Comfort*. **SPORTS**: Lake Placid, NY hosts the Winter Olympics. ✱ The U.S. boycotts the Moscow Summer Olympics. **FADS**: Rubick's Cube is introduced. **MISCELLANEOUS**: The Mariel Boatlift brings 125,000 Cuban refugees to the U.S. ✱ Mount St. Helens erupts in Washington state. **POPULATION**: The U.S. population is 226,542,203. ✱ 4,493,314 immigrants entered the U.S. during the previous decade.

1981

CATALOG *of Sources*

FAMILY *Milestones*

HISTORICAL *Context of 1981*

HEADLINE: The national debt surpasses one trillion dollars. **GOVERNMENT**: Iran releases its U.S. hostages. ✻ The Department of Agriculture tries to substitute ketchup for vegetables in school lunch programs. ✻ Reagan signs a bill which calls for the biggest tax cuts in U.S. history. ✻ Reagan authorizes CIA domestic operations. ✻ Sandra Day O'Connor becomes first woman on the Supreme Court. **MILITARY**: The U.S. shoots down two Libyan jets. **TRAGEDY**: Two aerial walkways at the Hyatt Regency Hotel in Kansas City, MO, collapse killing 113. **CRIME**: An assassination attempt on President Reagan fails. **LABOR**: Reagon fires 12,000 striking PATCO employees. **HEALTH**: The first U.S. test tube baby is born. ✻ More American women than men are smoking cigarettes. **EXPLORATION**: Space shuttle *Columbia* makes her maiden voyage. **NEW PRODUCTS**: IBM introduces the personal computer. ✻ VCRs become a household item. **BUSINESS**: GM reports its first loss since 1921. **BOOKS**: *Gorky Park* by Martin Cruz Smith; *Jumanji* by Chris van Allsburg. **ART**: Victor Ochoa paints the mural *Geronimo*. **MUSIC**: *Whip It*; *Coward of the County*; *Bette Davis Eyes*; *9 to 5*. **FILM**: *Raiders of the Lost Ark* with Harrison Ford; *Body Heat* with Kathleen Turner and William Hurt. **TV**: *Dynasty*; *Simon & Simon*; *Falcon Crest*; *Hill Street Blues*. ✻ MTV, the music video channel, begins broadcasting. **SPORTS**: Golfer Tom Watson wins the Masters Tournament. ✻ The Boston Celtics defeat the Houston Rockets for the NBA Championship. **FADS**: Jelly beans, Donkey Kong, Asteroids and Pac Man.

1982

FAMILY
Milestones

CATALOG *of Sources*

HEADLINE: Reagan announces a "war on drugs." **MILITARY**: U.S. Marines land in Lebanon on a peace keeping mission. **CRIME**: Tylenol is recalled after seven die from capsules laced with cyanide. **CIVIL RIGHTS**: The ERA is defeated. **EDUCATION**: Creationism no longer required to be taught in Arkansas schools. **HEALTH**: Barney Clark receives the first successful artificial heart. ✳ A connection between Reyes' Syndrome in children and aspirin established. ✳ Herpes reaches epidemic proportions. ✳ The FDA approves human insulin produced by bacteria. **SCIENCE**: The first successful gene transplant is performed in a mammal. **TRANSPORTATION**: The Boeing 767 makes its debut. **ECONOMICS**: Reagan signs a bill which removes "restraints" on S&Ls. **BOOKS**: *The Color Purple* by Alice Walker; *Mistral's Daughter* by Judith Krantz. **NEWSPAPERS**: The first national daily, *USA Today*, is launched. **THEATER**: *Little Shop of Horrors* by Menken and Ashman. **ART**: *Europe and the Jaguar* by Carlos Almaraz. **MUSIC**: *Ebony and Ivory*; *I Love Rock 'n Roll*; *Centerfold*; *Jack & Diane*. **FILM**: *E.T., The Extra-Terrestrial* by Steven Spielberg; *Victor/Victoria* with Julie Andrews; *Eating Raoul* with Paul Bartel. **TV**: *Cagney & Lacey*; *Cheers*; *Family Ties*; *Late Night with David Letterman*. **SPORTS**: The St. Louis Cardinals defeat the Milwaukee Brewers to take the World Series. ✳ The San Francisco 49ers defeat the Cincinnati Bengals to win the Super Bowl. **FADS**: Aerobic videos become popular. **NOTORIETY**: The Rev. Sun Myung Moon is sentenced to prison. **MISCELLANEOUS**: The Vietnam War Memorial is dedicated.

1983

FAMILY
Milestones

CATALOG *of Sources*

HEADLINE: A truck bomb kills 241 Marines in Beirut, Lebanon. **MILITARY**: Reagan proposes a "Strategic Defense Initiative" which is dubbed "Star Wars." ✳ U.S. forces invade Grenada. ✳ 63 die from a car bomb at the U.S. Embassy in Beirut. **CRIME**: Crack, a highly addictive form of cocaine, hits the streets. ✳ Scandals in the EPA force Rita M. Lavelle, James Watt and Anne McGill Burford to resign. **EDUCATION**: The National Commission on Excellence in Education publishes *A Nation at Risk*. **FOOD**: The sugar substitute, NutraSweet, is introduced. ✳ Caffeine-free colas are introduced. **COMMUNICATION**: AT&T is broken up into a long-distance company and "baby bells." **BOOKS**: *Gorillas in the Mist* by Diane Fossey; *Blue Highways* by William Least Heat Moon. **THEATER**: With 3,389 performances, *A Chorus Line* becomes the longest running show on Broadway. **ART**: *Surrounded Islands* by Christo. **MUSIC**: *Every Breath You Take*; *Billie Jean*; *Flashdance (What a Feeling)*. ✳ Michael Jackson releases the album *Thriller*. ✳ Recorded music becomes available on CDs. **DANCES**: Break dancing is popularized. **FILM**: *Koyaanisqatsi* by Godfrey Reggio; *Terms of Endearment* by James L. Brooks. **TV**: New shows include: *The A-Team*; *Wheel of Fortune*; *Night Court*. **FASHIONS**: Suspenders become fashionable for men. **SPORTS**: Martina Navratilova wins the women's U.S. Open in tennis. ✳ The Philadelphia 76ers defeat the Los Angeles Lakers for the NBA Championship. **FADS**: Cabbage Patch dolls peak in popularity. **OCCASIONS**: Martin Luther King, Jr.'s birthday becomes a national holiday. **MISCELLANEOUS**: The Soviet Union shoots down a Korean Air Lines 747 killing all 269 on board.

1984

CATALOG *of Sources*

FAMILY *Milestones*

HISTORICAL *Context of 1984*

HEADLINE: Ronald Reagan and George Bush are re-elected. **GOVERNMENT**: The Reagan administration cuts funding for international birth control programs. ✴ Geraldine Ferraro becomes the first woman to run for vice-president. **MILITARY**: The CIA covertly mines Nicaraguan harbors. ✴ A fund for Agent Orange victims is established. **CRIME**: Bernard Goetz defends himself against four youths in the New York City subway. ✴ Reports of alleged child abuse at some day-care centers causes hysteria. ✴ Twenty-two are killed in a shooting at a McDonald's in San Ysidro, CA. **HEALTH**: The AIDS virus is identified. **RELIGION**: Southern Baptist convention opposes the ordination of women. **SCIENCE**: Astronomers observe a distant solar system being formed. **NEW PRODUCTS**: Apple introduces the "user-friendly" Macintosh personal computer. **ECONOMICS**: The U.S. becomes a debtor nation. **BOOKS**: *The Unbearable Lightness of Being* by Milan Kundera; *Pieces of My Mind* by Andy Rooney. **MUSIC**: *Hello; Time After Time; Footloose; What's Love Got to Do With It?; Missing You.* ✴ Madonna's album *Like A Virgin* is released. **FILM**: *Amadeus* with Tom Hulce and F. Murray Abraham; *Beverly Hills Cop* with Eddie Murphy. **TV**: *Hunter; Murder, She Wrote; The Bill Cosby Show; Miami Vice.* **SPORTS**: The Soviets and some other nations boycott the Olympics at Los Angeles. ✴ The Detroit Tigers defeat the San Diego Padres to take the World Series. **FADS**: The board game *Trivial Pursuit* and the Teenage Mutant Ninja Turtles becomes fads. **NOTORIETY**: Vanessa Williams is forced to give up her Miss America crown. **MISCELLANEOUS**: Jesse Jackson gains the release of an American Navy pilot held by Syria.

1985

CATALOG *of Sources*

FAMILY
Milestones

HEADLINE: TOW missiles are secretly delivered to Iran. **CRIME**: Philadelphia police firebomb the headquarters of MOVE. ✷ John Walker, his son, and brother are arrested for espionage. **ECOLOGY**: Leaded gasoline banned. ✷ Federal tax credits for home solar installations are discontinued. **EXPLORATION**: The wreck of the *Titanic* is found. **SCIENCE**: Carbon fullerenes, "bucky balls," a new form of pure carbon is discovered. **INVENTIONS**: The scanning-tunneling microscope is developed. **FOOD**: Due to popular demand Coca-Cola brings back its original formula as *Classic Coke*. **ECONOMICS**: World oil prices collapse and banks heavily invested in oil production fail. **BUSINESS**: Montgomery Ward discontinues its mail-order catalog. **BOOKS**: *The Accidental Tourist* by Anne Tyler; *Elvis and Me* by Priscilla Presley; *Sarah, Plain and Tall* by Patricia MacLachlan; *The Polar Express* by Chris van Allsburg. **MUSIC**: *Say You, Say Me*; *Careless Whisper*; *Material Girl*; *Shout*; *We Are the World*. ✷ "Live Aid," a rock benefit for Africa. ✷ Compact discs begin to replace vinyl records. **FILM**: *Cocoon* by Ron Howard; *The Color Purple* with Whoopi Goldberg; *Kiss of the Spider Woman* with William Hurt; *Out of Africa* with Meryl Streep and Robert Redford. **TV**: *Golden Girls*; *The Oprah Winfrey Show*. **FASHIONS**: Shoulder pads reappear in women's fashions. **SPORTS**: Ivan Lendl wins the U.S. Open in tennis. ✷ The San Francisco 49ers defeat the Miami Dolphins to win the Super Bowl. **FADS**: "Baby on Board" signs appear in car rear windows. **MISCELLANEOUS**: The cartoon strip, "Calvin and Hobbes," debuts.

1986

CATALOG *of Sources*

FAMILY *Milestones*

HISTORICAL *Context of 1986*

HEADLINE: The space shuttle *Challenger* explodes killing all on board. **GOVERNMENT**: The U.S. trades Iran arms for hostages. * Congress restructures the federal income tax system. * The Iran-Contra Affair is exposed. **MILITARY**: U.S. warplanes bomb Muammar Qadaffi's headquarters in Tripoli. **CRIME**: Random drug-testing is introduced to certain sensitive jobs. **CIVIL RIGHTS**: The U.S. Supreme Court upholds affirmative-action hiring quotas to favor women and minorities. **ECOLOGY**: A hole in the Earth's ozone layer is discovered over Antarctica. **SCIENCE**: A superconducting ceramic is developed. **BUSINESS**: Thousands of small U.S. farmers go bankrupt. * Wall Street is scandalized by revelations of insider trading. **BOOKS**: *Kristy's Great Idea* by Ann Martin; *The Handmaid's Tale* by Margaret Atwood; *Fatherhood* by Bill Cosby. **MUSIC**: *That's What Friends Are For*; *Walk Like an Egyptian*; *On My Way*; *Greatest Love of All*; *Rock Me Amadeus*; *Living in America* * *The Broadway Album* by Barbra Streisand. **FILM**: *Down and Out in Beverly Hills* with Bette Midler; *Aliens* with Sigourney Weaver; *Little Shop of Horrors* by Frank Oz; *Platoon* by Oliver Stone. **TV**: *Family Ties*; *L.A. Law*; *Matlock*; *Alf*. * The FOX TV network begins operations. **FASHIONS**: Denim skirts and dresses are fashionable. **SPORTS**: Jack Nicklaus wins the U.S. Open. * Mike Tyson wins the heavyweight title. * The Chicago Bears defeat the New England Patriots to win the Super Bowl. **FADS**: Nintendo video games are debuted. **MISCELLANEOUS**: During Hands Across America, 5.4 million people form a chain from New York City, NY, to Long Beach, CA.

1987

FAMILY
Milestones

CATALOG *of Sources*

HISTORICAL *Context of 1987*

HEADLINE: Jim Bakker resigns his PTL ministry after a sexual liaison with church secretary Jessica Hahn. **GOVERNMENT**: Gary Hart's presidential campaign ends after allegations of sexual impropriety with Donna Rice on a boat named *Monkey Business*. ✳ The U.S. Supreme Court upholds the right of the Cabazon Reservation to hold high-stakes bingo games. ✳ Hearings on Iran-Contra and the Wedtech Scandal. **MILITARY**: Soviet premier Gorbachev and President Reagan sign an arms reduction treaty. ✳ America sends forces to the Persian Gulf to protect oil shipments. **HEALTH**: Tobacco smoking restrictions become commonplace. **RELIGION**: New Agers celebrate "harmonic convergence" as the planets align. **SCIENCE**: Genetically engineered bacteria, to control frost, are open-air tested. ✳ A ceramic superconductor which conducts at -238° C is discovered. **COMMUNICATION**: New Jersey Bell offers "Caller ID." **ECONOMICS**: The Dow drops 508 points in one day. **BOOKS**: *Patriot Games* by Tom Clancy; *The Bonfire of the Vanities* by Tom Wolf; *A Day in the Life of America* by Rick Smolan. **THEATER**: *Into the Woods* by Stephen Sondheim. **MUSIC**: *Faith*; *Alone*; *La Bamba*; *I Wanna Dance With Somebody*. ✳ Album: *Licensed to Ill* by the Beastie Boys. **RADIO**: *National Native News* debuts. **FILM**: *The Last Emperor* by Bernardo Bertolucci; *Moonstruck* with Cher; *Full Metal Jacket* by Stanley Kubrick. **TV**: *Beauty and the Beast*; *Ducktales*; *A Different World*; *Star Trek: The Next Generation*. **SPORTS**: The Minnesota Twins defeat the St. Louis Cardinals to take the World Series. ✳ The Los Angeles Lakers defeat the Boston Celtics for the NBA Championship.

1988

FAMILY
Milestones

CATALOG *of Sources*

HEADLINE: George Bush and Dan Quayle are elected president and VP. **MILITARY**: The B-2 Stealth bomber is unveiled. **TRAGEDY**: The *U.S.S. Vincennes* shoots down an Iranian airbus killing 290 people. ✳ 247 die when a Pan Am Boeing 747 is blown up by a terrorist bomb over Lockerbie, Scotland. **CRIME**: The BCCI scandal unfolds. ✳ Michael Milken, "junk bond" dealer, pleads guilty to felony charges. **CIVIL RIGHTS**: The U.S. formally apologizes for the WWII internment of Japanese-Americans. **HEALTH**: Studies determine that an aspirin-a-day reduces the risk of heart attack. ✳ The FDA approves minoxidil for baldness. **RELIGION**: Evangelist Jimmy Swaggart is defrocked and banned from TV. **SCIENCE**: Harvard scientists obtain a patent for a genetically engineered mouse. **BOOKS**: *A Brief History of Time* by Stephen Hawking; *The Icarus Agenda* by Robert Ludlum. **MAGAZINES**: The English language magazine *Hispanic* is founded. **THEATER**: *The Phantom of the Opera* by Andrew Lloyd Webber. **MUSIC**: *Roll With It*; *One More Try*; *Sweet Child o' Mine*; *Simply Irresistible*. **FILM**: *Who Framed Roger Rabbit?* by Roger Zemeckis; *Stand and Deliver* by Ramon Menedez. **TV**: Bill Moyers hosts *Joseph Campbell and the Power of Myth*. ✳ *Murphy Brown*; *Roseanne*; *Thirtysomething*; *The Wonder Years*. **SPORTS**: The Los Angeles Dodgers defeat the Oakland Athletics to take the World Series. ✳ The Los Angeles Lakers defeat the Detroit Pistons for the NBA Championship. **FADS**: The Koosh Ball is a popular new toy. ✳ Karaoke comes to the U.S. **MISCELLANEOUS**: White House aide Donald Regan states that Nancy Reagan uses astrology to plan her husband's activities.

1989

CATALOG *of Sources*

FAMILY *Milestones*

HISTORICAL *Context of 1989*

HEADLINE: The multi-billion dollar bail out of the failed S&Ls begins. **GOVERNMENT**: President Bush announces another "war on drugs." **MILITARY**: American forces invade Panama to capture General Noriega. **TRAGEDY**: Hurricane Hugo devastates parts of the East Coast. ✴ San Francisco is struck by a severe earthquake. **CIVIL RIGHTS**: The National American Indian Museum Act requires the return of Indian remains to their tribes. ✴ The Supreme Court rules that burning the U.S. flag to protest government policies is a protected right. **ECOLOGY**: The grounded tanker *Exxon Valdez* spills oil into Prince William Sound, AK. **SCIENCE**: A "cold-fusion" discovery at the University of Utah is a flop. **FOOD**: "Dry" beers are introduced. **BOOKS**: *The Joy Luck Club* by Amy Tan; *The Satanic Verses* by Salman Rushdie; *Number the Stars* by Lois Lowry. **ART**: Robert Mapplethorpe's photography stirs up controversy. **MUSIC**: *Miss You Much*; *Straight Up*; *Lost in Your Eyes*; *Wind Beneath My Wings*. ✴ *The Raw and the Cooked*, an album by Fine Young Cannibals, is released. **FILM**: *The Adventures of Baron Munchhausen* by Terry Gilliam; *Batman* with Michael Keaton, Jack Nicholson and Kim Basinger; *Do the Right Thing* by Spike Lee; *Driving Miss Daisy* with Jessica Tandy and Morgan Freeman. **TV**: *Life Goes On*; *Anthing But Love*; *The Simpsons*. **SPORTS**: Nolan Ryan pitches his 5,000th strikeout. ✴ The Detroit Pistons defeat the Los Angeles Lakers for the NBA Championship. **FADS**: Teenage Mutant Ninja Turtles are favorites with small boys. **NOTORIETY**: Leona Helmsley is convicted of income tax evasion and tax fraud.

1990

FAMILY
Milestones

CATALOG *of Sources*

HISTORICAL *Context of 1990*

HEADLINE: The U.S. leads Operation Desert Shield after Iraq invades Kuwait. **CRIME**: Investigations into the "Keating Five." **CIVIL RIGHTS**: The Americans with Disabilities Act is signed. **EDUCATION**: Home schooling is popularized. **HEALTH**: The FDA approves the Norplant contraceptive. ✴ A girl is the first human treated with gene therapy. **RELIGION**: The Supreme Court rules that Native Americans may be prosecuted for using peyote in religious ceremonies. ✴ Reform Judaism adopts a policy that sanctions homosexual behavior. ✴ Sex scandals involve the Roman Catholic clergy. **ECOLOGY**: Killer bees enter the U.S. **SCIENCE**: The National Center for Human Genome Research is created. ✴ Researchers grow human brain cells in the laboratory. **FOOD**: Benzene contamination forces *Perrier* to recall millions of bottles. **BOOKS**: *Buffalo Girls* by Larry McMurty; *Iron John* by Robert Bly. **MUSIC**: *Vision of Love*; *Opposites Attract*; *It Must Have Been Love*. **FILM**: *Henry & June* by Philip Kaufman; *Mountains of the Moon* by Bob Rafelson; *Edward Scissorhands* with Johnny Depp. **TV**: *Beverly Hills 90210*; *Northern Exposure*; *America's Funniest Home Videos*; *In Living Color*; *Law & Order*. ✴ *The Civil War*, a PBS special by Ken Burns. **FASHIONS**: Leggings and miniskirts are popular. **SPORTS**: The Detroit Pistons defeat the Portland Trailblazers for the NBA championship. **FADS**: Bungee jumping and Vietnamese potbellied pigs as pets are popularized. **MISCELLANEOUS**: After years of court battles, Gilbert Hyatt receives a patent for a microprocessor. **POPULATION**: The U.S. population is 248,709,873. ✴ 7,338,062 immigrants entered the U.S. in the previous decade.

1991

FAMILY *Milestones*

CATALOG *of Sources*

HEADLINE: The ground war phase of Operation Desert Storm ends in 100 hours with Iraqi forces defeated. **MILITARY**: The Tailhook Convention in Las Vegas exposes sexual harassment in the U.S. Navy. **CRIME**: LAPD officers are videotaped beating Rodney King. ✷ Officers of BCCI are indicted on criminal charges. **LABOR**: San Francisco enacts laws regulating working conditions at video display terminals. **EDUCATION**: Bush unveils *Goals: 2000*. **INVENTIONS**: Texas Instruments produces the first OEIC (optoelectrical integrated circuit) chip. **BOOKS**: *The Firm* by John Grisham; *The Kitchen God's Wife* by Amy Tan. **MUSIC**: *Black or White*; *All 4 Love*; *Romantic*; *Fading Like a Flower*; *Emotions*; *Every Heartbeat*. **RADIO**: *The Rush Limbaugh Show* becomes popular. **FILM**: *The Addams Family* with Angelica Huston and Raul Julia; *Point Break* by Kathryn Bigelow; *Thelma and Louise* with Geena Davis and Susan Sarandon. **TV**: *Taz-Mania*; *Herman's Head*; *Step by Step*; *Home Improvement*; *I'll Fly Away*. **FASHIONS**: Sports sandals are popularized. **SPORTS**: The Minneapolis Twins defeat the Atlanta Braves to take the World Series. ✷ The Washington Redskins defeat the Buffalo Bills to win the Super Bowl. **FADS**: Kids creatively employ Super-Soaker water guns. **NOTORIETY**: Clarence Thomas is appointed to the U.S. Supreme Court amid controversy over charges of sexual harassment by a former coworker. ✷ Bush comes under attack for encouraging Kurdish and Shi'ite revolt in Iraq and then not supporting it. **MISCELLANEOUS**: The Bureau of Engraving and Printing makes paper currency more difficult to counterfeit. ✷ The Custer Battlefield National Monument is renamed the Little Bighorn Battlefield National Monument.

1992

CATALOG *of Sources*

FAMILY
Milestones

HISTORICAL *Context of 1992*

HEADLINE: Riots follow the acquittal of 4 white LAPD officers in the beating of Rodney King. **GOVERNMENT**: Four persons die in the shoot-out at Ruby Ridge, ID. ✳ Bush pardons officials for lying to Congress about the Iran-Contra affair. ✳ Bill Clinton and Al Gore are elected President and VP **MILITARY**: Pentagon authorizes a DNA identification system. ✳ U.S. troops are sent to Somalia. **TRAGEDY**: Hurricane Andrew leaves 250,000 homeless in Florida. **HEALTH**: FDA approves Taxol to fight ovarian cancer. ✳ FDA bans silicone breast implants. **SCIENCE**: Comets are observed at the edge of the solar system in the Kuiper belt. ✳ The newest atomic clock loses only one second in 1.6 million years. ✳ Genetically engineered plants produce biodegradable plastic. **NEW PRODUCTS**: Kodak introduces photo CDs. **FOOD**: Industrial lasers are developed to peel fruits and vegetables. **ECONOMICS**: The U.S., Canada and Mexico sign the North American Free Trade Agreement. ✳ The national debt tops $3 trillion. **BUSINESS**: The world's largest shopping mall opens in Bloomington, MN. **BOOKS**: *Vox* by Nicholas Baker; *Morning Girl* by Michael Dorris. **MUSIC**: *I Will Always Love You*; *I'll Be There*; *November Rain*; *Baby Got Back*; *Jump*; *Achy Breaky Heart*. **FILM**: *Bram Stoker's Dracula* by Francis Ford Coppola; *The Lawnmower Man* by Brett Leonard. **TV**: *Mad About You*; *Melrose Place*; *The Young Indiana Jones Chronicles*. ✳ Dan Quayle debates a fictional Murphy Brown over "family values." **SPORTS**: The Toronto Blue Jays defeat the Atlanta Braves to take the World Series. **FADS**: Barney, the purple dinosaur, is popular with pre-kindergarteners.

1993

CATALOG *of Sources*

FAMILY *Milestones*

CATALOG *of Sources*

HEADLINE: Eight Muslim extremists are arrested for involvement in the World Trade Center bombing in New York. **MILITARY**: After $30 billion, "Star Wars" (the Strategic Defense Initiative) is canceled. ✴ U.S. troops are pulled out of Somalia. **TRAGEDY**: Flooding along the Mississippi and Missouri rivers causes billions in damage. **CRIME**: Dozens die when the ATF attempts a raid on the Branch Davidian compound at Waco, TX. ✴ Several foreign tourists are murdered in Miami, FL. ✴ Dr. David Gunn is shot in the back and killed by a "Right to Life" extremist. **EDUCATION**: A survey of the American workforce finds one-half is unfit for employment. **HEALTH**: Hantavirus deaths cause fear in the Southwest. ✴ A cryptosporidum outbreak in Milwaukee's drinking water supply makes thousands ill. **EXPLORATION**: After two years the occupants of Biosphere 2 emerge from their structure. **SCIENCE**: The first test of the Delta Clipper rocket is successful. ✴ The orbiting Hubble telescope is repaired. ✴ Human embryos are successfully cloned. **BUSINESS**: Sears Roebuck discontinues its general merchandise catalog. **BOOKS**: *The Client* by John Grisham; *Healing and the Mind* by Bill Moyers; *Bridges of Madison County* by Robert James Waller. **MUSIC**: *That's the Way Love Goes*; *Dreamlover*; *I'm Every Woman*; *Ordinary World*. **DANCES**: Country line-dancing is popularized. **FILM**: *Made in America* with Whoopi Goldberg and Ted Danson; *Schindler's List* by Steven Spielberg. **TV**: *NYPD Blue*; *Grace Under Fire*; *John Larroquette Show*; *The Adventures of Brisco County, Jr.*; *Dr. Quinn, Medicine Woman*; *Animaniacs*. **SPORTS**: The Toronto Blue Jays defeat the Philadelphia Phillies to take the World Series.

1994

FAMILY
Milestones

CATALOG *of Sources*

HEADLINE: The GOP wins control of both houses for the first time in 40 years. **MILITARY**: U.S. troops intervene in Haiti. **TRAGEDY**: 14 smoke jumpers are killed on Colorado's Storm King Mountain. **CRIME**: Violence associated with cigarette smuggling along the U.S. border forces Canada to lower its tobacco tax. ✶ CIA agent Aldrich Ames is convicted of spying for the Soviet Union. **LABOR**: United Airline employees become majority shareholders. **RELIGION**: A white buffalo, sacred to Native Americans, is born. **ECOLOGY**: The California Desert Protection Act becomes law. **SCIENCE**: Confirmation of planets beyond our solar system. **INVENTIONS**: Transistors containing no metallic parts are developed. **COMMUNICATION**: The new Intelink network allows spy agencies to access secret information from almost anywhere. **ECONOMICS**: 15 percent of families live below the poverty line. **BOOKS**: *The Celestine Prophecy* by James Redfield; *Magic Eye* by Thomas Baccei. **MUSIC**: *Always*; *All for Love*; *Breathe Again*; *I'll Remember*; *Return to Innocence*. ✶ 350,000 celebrate the 25th anniversary of Woodstock at Saugerties, NY. **FILM**: *The Flintstones* by Paul Weiland; *Forrest Gump* by Robert Zemeckis; *The Mask* with Jim Carrey. **TV**: *Party of Five*; *Friends*; *ER*; *Due South*; *Ellen*. ✶ Time-Warner introduces an interactive TV system. **SPORTS**: The World Series is canceled due to a player strike. ✶ The U.S. Soccer team advances to the second round of the World Cup playoffs. ✶ Ice skater Nancy Kerrigan is injured by an attacker. **NOTORIETY**: American Michael Fay is caned in Singapore for acts of defacement. **MISCELLANEOUS**: Thousands of Cubans and Haitians escape to the U.S.

1995

CATALOG *of Sources*

FAMILY *Milestones*

HEADLINE: U.S. troops are deployed as peacekeepers in the Balkans. **GOVERNMENT**: Republican Senator Bob Packwood resigns from the Senate amid sexual harassment charges. **MILITARY**: In his book, *In Retrospect: The Tragedy and Lessons of Vietnam*, Robert McNamara calls the Vietnam War a grave mistake. **CRIME**: O.J. Simpson is acquitted of the murder of his ex-wife Nicole Simpson and Ronald Goldman. ✳ Tejano singer, Selena, is killed by the former president of her fan club. **EDUCATION**: *The Manufactured Crisis: Myths, Fraud, and the Attack on America's Public Schools* by Addison Wesley. **HEALTH**: Melatonin is touted as the drug to a better, more energetic and longer life. **RELIGION**: Louis Farrakhan, of the Nations of Islam, spearheads a Million Man March on Washington, DC. **SCIENCE**: A new state of matter is created: the Bose-Einstein condensate. ✳ A solar-powered airplane attains an altitude of 15,400 meters. **INVENTIONS**: An electromagnetic gun detector is under development. **TRANSPORTATION**: The federal government allows states to set their own speed limits on interstate highways. **BUSINESS**: The closing of Smith Corona marks the end of the typewriter era. **BOOKS**: *My American Journey* by Colin Powell; *Emotional Intelligence* by Daniel Coleman. **MUSIC**: *Take a Bow*; *On Bended Knee*; *Another Night*; *Candy Rain*; *Red Light Special*. **RADIO**: *Blacklisted* by Tony Kahn is broadcast on NPR. **FILM**: *Apollo 13* by Ron Howard; *Clueless* by Amy Heckerling; *Jumanji* with Robin Williams. **TV**: *The Jeff Foxworthy Show*; *Murder One*; *Mad TV*; *The Drew Carey Show*. **SPORTS**: The San Francisco 49ers defeat the San Diego Chargers in the Super Bowl.

1996

CATALOG *of Sources*

FAMILY
Milestones

HISTORICAL *Context of 1996*

1997

FAMILY
Milestones

CATALOG *of Sources*

1998

FAMILY
Milestones

CATALOG *of Sources*

HISTORICAL *Context of 1998*

HISTORICAL Context of 1998

1999

FAMILY
Milestones

CATALOG *of Sources*

HISTORICAL *Context of 1999*

2000

CATALOG *of Sources*

FAMILY *Milestones*

HISTORICAL *Context of 2000*

BIBLIOGRAPHY

Books of general facts:

Grun, Bernard (1991). *The Timetables of History*: A Horizontal Linkage of People and Events. Simon & Schuster, New York, NY.

Slavens, Thomas P. (1990). *Number One in the U.S.A.*: Records and Wins in Sports, Entertainment, Business, and Science, With Sources Cited. Scarecrow Press, Metuchen, NJ.

Wenborn, Neil (1991). *The U.S.A., A Chronicle in Pictures*. Smithmark, Westlake Village, CA.

Books of general facts with explanations:

Carruth, Gorton (1987). *The Encyclopedia of American Facts & Dates*, Harper & Row, New York, NY.

Facts on File. Facts on File, Inc., New York, NY.

Marsh, Earle (1988). *The Complete Directory to Prime Time Network TV Shows, 1946 to present*. Ballantine Books, New York, NY.

Trager, James (1994). *The People's Chronology*: A Year-by-year Record of Human Events from Prehistory to the Present. Holt, New York, NY.

Urdang, Laurence (1981). *The Timetables of American History*. Simon & Schuster, New York, NY.

Wallace, Irving (1980). *The People's Almanac Presents the Book of Lists #2*. Morrow, New York, NY.

Special topic books:

Association for Library Service to Children (1995). *The Newberry and Caldecott Awards*: A Guide to the Medal and Honor Books. American Library Association, Chicago, IL.

Erickson, Hal (1995). *Television Cartoon Shows*: An Illustrated Encyclopedia, 1949 through 1993. McFarland, Jefferson City, NC.

Gardner, Martin (1957). *Fads and Fallacies in the Name of Science*. Dover Publications, New York, NY.

Hoffmann, Frank W. (1994). *Fashion and Merchandising Fads*. Haworth Press, New York, NY.

Kanellos, Nicolas (1994). *The Hispanic Almanac*: From Columbus to Corporate America. Invisible Ink, Detroit, MI.

Rood, Karen Lane (1994). *American Culture After World War II*. Gale Research, Detroit, MI.

Sann, Paul (1967). *Fads, Follies, and Delusions of the American People*. Crown Publishers, New York, NY.

Stern, Jane (1992). *Jane & Micael Stern's Encyclopedia of Pop Culture*: An A to Z guide of Who's Who and What's What, from Aerobics and Bubble Gum to Valley of the Dolls and Moon Unit Zappa. Harper Perennial, New York, NY.

Popular history books:

Time-Life Books (1969-70). *This Fabulous Century*. New York, NY.

Magazines:

Variety. Variety Publishing Co., New York, NY.

More Great Books Full of Great Ideas!

The Unpuzzling Your Past Workbook: Essential Forms and Letters for All Genealogists—Now unpuzzling your past is easier than ever using 42 genealogical forms designed to make organizing, searching, record-keeping and presenting information effortless. *#70327/$15.99/320 pages/paperback*

Unpuzzling Your Past: A Basic Guide to Genealogy—Make uncovering your roots easy with this complete genealogical research guide. You'll find everything you need—handy forms, sample letters and worksheets, census extraction forms, a comprehensive resource section, bibliographies and case studies. Plus, updated information on researching courthouse records, federal government resources and computers on genealogy. *#70301/$14.99/180 pages/paperback*

Writing Family Histories and Memoirs—From conducting solid research to writing a compelling book, this guide will help you recreate your past. Polking will help you determine what type of book to write, why you are writing the book and what its scope should be. Plus, you'll find writing samples, memory triggers and more! *#70295/$14.99/272 pages*

Families Writing—Here is a book that details why and how to record words that go straight to the heart—the simple, vital words that will speak to those you care most about and to their descendants many years from now. *#10294/$14.99/198 pages/paperback*

How to Write the Story of Your Life—Leave a record of your life for generations to come! This book makes memoir writing an enjoyable undertaking—even if you have little or no writing experience. Spiced with plenty of encouragement to keep you moving your story towards completion. *#10132/$13.99/230 pages/paperback*

Turning Life into Fiction—Learn how to turn your life, those of friends and family members, and newspaper accounts into fictional novels and short stories. Through insightful commentary and hands-on exercises, you'll hone the essential skills of creating fiction from journal entries, identifying the memories ripest for development, ethically fictionalizing other people's sto-ries, gaining distance from personal experience and much more. *#48000/$17.99/208 pages*

How to Have a 48-Hour Day—Get more done and have more fun as you double what you can do in a day! Aslett reveals reasons to be more productive everywhere— and what "production" actually is. You'll learn how to keep accomplishing despite setbacks, ways to boost effectiveness, the things that help your productivity and much more. *#70339/$12.99/160 pages/120 illus./paperback*

Make Your House Do the Housework, Revised Edition—Take advantage of new work-saving products, materials and approaches to make your house keep itself in order. You'll discover page after page of practical, environmentally-friendly new ideas and methods for minimizing home cleaning and maintenance. This book includes charts that rate materials and equipment. Plus, you'll find suggestions for approaching everything from simple do-it-yourself projects to remodeling jobs of all sizes. *#70293/$14.99/208 pages/215 b&w illus./paperback*

Stephanie Culp's 12-Month Organizer and Project Planner—The projects you're burning to start or yearning to finish will zoom toward accomplishment by using these forms, "To-Do" lists, checklists and calendars. Culp helps you break any project into manageable segments, set deadlines, establish plans and follow them—step by attainable step. *#70274/$12.99/192 pages/paperback*

Don't Be A Slave to Housework—Busy people—learn how to get your house in order and keep it that way. From quick cleanups to hiring help, this book is loaded with advice! *#70273/$10.99/176 pages/paperback*

Don Aslett's Clutter-Free! Finally and Forever—Free yourself of unnecessary stuff that chokes your home and clogs your life! If you feel owned by your belongings, you'll discover incredible excuses people use for allowing clutter, how to beat the "no- time" excuse, how to determine what's junk, how to prevent recluttering and much more! *#70306/$12.99/224 pages/50 illus./paperback*

You Can Find More Time for Yourself Every Day—Professionals, working mothers, college students—if you're in a hurry, you need this time-saving guide! Quizzes, tests and charts will show you how to make the most of your minutes! *#70258/$12.99/208 pages/paperback*

Confessions of a Happily Organized Family—Learn how to make your mornings peaceful, chores more fun and mealtime more relaxing by getting the whole family organized. *#01145/$10.99/248 pages/paperback*

Clutter's Last Stand—You think you're organized, yet closets bulge around you. Get out of clutter denial with loads of practical advice. *#01122/$11.99/280 pages/paperback*

The Organization Map—You *will* defeat disorganization. This effective guide is chock full of tips for time-management, storage solutions and more! *#70224/$12.99/208 pages/paperback*

Office Clutter Cure—Discover how to clear out office clutter— overflowing "in" boxes, messy desks and bulging filing cabinets. Don Aslett offers a cure for every kind of office clutter that hinders productivity— even mental clutter like gossip and office politics. *#70296/$9.99/192 pages/175 illus./paperback*

It's Here . . . Somewhere—Need help getting and keeping your busy household in order? This book provides step-by-step instruction on how to get more places out of spaces with a room-by-room approach to organization. *#10214/$10.99/192 pages/50 b&w illus./paperback*

Slow Down and Get More Done—Discover precisely the right pace for your life by gaining control of worry, making possibilities instead of plans and learning the value of doing "nothing." *#70183/$12.99/192 pages/paperback*

How to Get Organized When You Don't Have the Time—You keep meaning to organize the closet and clean out the garage, but who has the time? Culp combines proven time-management principles with practical ideas to help you clean-up key trouble spots in a hurry. *#01354/$11.99/216 pages/paperback*